EFFORTLESS CASH FLOW

EFFORTLESS CASH FLOW

The ABC's of TICs
(Tenant in Common properties)

Kathy Heshelow

iUniverse, Inc.
New York   Bloomington   Shanghai

Effortless Cash Flow
The ABC's of TICs (Tenant in Common properties)

iUniverse books may be ordered through booksellers or by contacting:

iUniverse
1663 Liberty Drive
Bloomington, IN 47403
www.iuniverse.com
1-800-Authors (1-800-288-4677)

Because of the dynamic nature of the Internet, any Web addresses or links contained in this book may have changed since publication and may no longer be valid.

The views expressed in this work are solely those of the author and do not necessarily reflect the views of the publisher, and the publisher hereby disclaims any responsibility for them.

Third Edition, April 2008

ISBN: 978-0-595-38539-3 (pbk)
ISBN: 978-0-595-82917-0 (ebk)

Printed in the United States of America

I dedicate this book to my husband, Harlan.

Contents

List of Photographs

The photos in this book represent TIC properties that were purchased in 2005 or previous as TICs. They are included to give the reader an idea as to the caliber of the typical TIC investment.

List of Figures

Acknowledgments

I would like to thank all of the TIC sponsors who have provided photos for this book. I'm sorry I couldn't accommodate everyone this time.

Everything starts with the sponsor. Without them, the investor would have nothing to buy and there would be no TIC industry! The sponsors certainly have much responsibility upon their heads, including searching out the right properties, conducting extensive due diligence, going through the extensive securitization process and structuring them correctly for the investors, signing for loans, and so forth. They then follow through with the investors for years.

I would like to thank tax attorney, Robert Sommers, for allowing me to reference some of his historical information about the 1031 tax-deferred exchange for this book. I would like to thank Tim Cronic for his time and expertise on the 1031 process. Thanks to Manuel Nogales of Omni Consulting & Research for the Exit Strategy Statistics as well as for the TIC statistics. Thanks to Amy Knickerbocker at A3K Design. I would like to thank Shanon Ford at PacWest for the large packet of information on Best Practices materials and supporting documents. Thanks to David Levine of Private Placement Market for his insights. Thanks also to Joe Downs at DeSanto. Finally, I thank CapWest Securities for their support.

Introduction

Welcome to the world of specialized real estate investment!

You are about to discover what the Tenant in Common (TIC) industry is all about. Certainly, those of us in this industry find it exciting and dynamic. However, due to their structure, TICs are somewhat complicated. To the uninitiated, they can also be confusing. However, many of my clients who invested have often come back to me and said, "I wish I had known about these types of investments before. Cash flow without management!" Of course, these investments are not for everyone, and should not be for everyone, based on financial situation and suitability. This will be explained.

This book is an introductory primer to help those contemplating a TIC investment. As will be explained, TICs are a complex weaving together of the worlds of commercial real estate, securities, finance and law. However, this book is neither a law treatise nor a definitive work by any means. I could spend many more pages of detail on each subject treated in the book, especially securities law, deeper issues on TICs themselves, and tax issues. However, the intent is to give a basic overview of the subject and not to put new investors into a deep sleep!

The TIC world is young, but it is quickly maturing. By the end of 2005 and beginning in 2006, we had a larger number offerings available for investors than ever before. Typically, when a new TIC offering came out, it could be full within a matter of several days—even hours. There were not enough offerings for the many interested investors. Compared to other types of real estate, one does make faster decisions with this type of investment. Because many investors are conducting 1031 tax-deferred exchanges, the timing is relatively short for investors anyway. Today, while there is still urgency and demand for TICs, investors and their advisors have more choice and time to review the array of offerings. The supply and demand has evened out.

I would like to offer a word about terms used in the book. There are many formats used for Tenant in Common, Tenancy in common and TIC. (Specifically, the hyphenation and capitalization can vary.) When discussing the property itself in this book, I use the words "Tenant in Common" or "TIC." When discussing the investors into such property, I use the words "tenants-in-common." I thought this would help alleviate some confusion and make some visual distinctions as you read and absorb the information. I have included a glossary at the end of the book, which may be helpful for the various terms of law, real estate and finance you will encounter.

This book represents my opinion and reporting of facts. I am not an attorney, accountant, securities expert, lender, tax expert or qualified intermediary. I am a commercial real estate broker with experience in all types of real estate. I specialize in triple-net (NNN) properties, often for those in a 1031 tax-deferred exchange. I am also a licensed securities representative for private and public placements. In this book, I provide the best information available on TICs and related subjects for educational purposes. However, specific details, as they apply to you or your tax situation, should be discussed with your attorney, accountant or other specialist. While the information included is as accurate as possible, it is not warranted.

I hope you will both learn about this complicated investment type and enjoy the book as well. You may contact me with questions or comments at legacykathy@aol.com, toll free at 866-891-1031, or use the 'Contact Me' icon at www.tic-investments.org.

Kathy Heshelow

This book represents neither an offer to sell nor a solicitation to buy a security. Such an offer can only be made by means of a Private Placement Memorandum.

Photo 1. Sponsor: Triple Net Properties, LLC. 123 North Wacker Drive, Chicago, Illinois.

Chapter 1

What Are Tenant-in-Common (TIC) Properties? Why Are They So Popular?

Maybe you have heard about Tenant in Common (TIC) investments, or maybe you have heard snippets of information about them. Maybe you are doing a 1031 tax-deferred exchange and someone suggested a TIC to you. Maybe you tried an Internet search and found all sorts of references to TICs but not much detailed information. Maybe you have spoken with a few people and are thinking about investing but feel you need to know more. You might think TICs have been one of the best-kept secrets of recent years. In any case, you are certainly curious to know more about these investments. That's why you have this book!

What is a TIC?

The term "tenants in common" is a definition in law and real estate and refers to a way real estate is held. The legal dictionary defines tenants in common as a legal arrangement whereby two individuals or more can share ownership of a property. Unlike joint tenancy, tenancy in common allows a deceased person's property or property share to be passed to his or her beneficiaries instead of to the other owner(s). The property is held in common or in indivision.

What has evolved is an industry in which large, prepackaged, professionally-managed, institutional-grade properties, such as office buildings, shopping centers, or apartment complexes, are being offered by sponsors as Tenant in Common (TIC) properties. Each investor or co-owner obtains a percentage interest, or fractional interest, with all rights of possession and ownership. However, each investor or co-owner is not involved in the day-to-day management. Each TIC investor enjoys his or her pro rata share of the net income, tax shelters, non-recourse loan, appreciation, and share of the proceeds at the property's resale. The investor into this type of TIC would, in fact, be holding the real estate as a tenants-in-common.

These professionally packaged properties are passive income vehicles with a cash flow paid monthly. These are not partnerships, general or limited. Today's TICs are usually formed as a limited liability company (LLC). You, the investor, have voting power on key decisions. In addition to office buildings, shopping centers and apartment complexes—the "three main food groups" commonly offered—other asset types such as assisted-living facilities, golf courses, hotels, or industrial properties are occasionally offered.

To be clear: while you could join with college friends or relatives to buy a piece of local property and hold title to that property as tenants-in-common, this book is discussing the institutional-grade properties that are sold to investors around the country (usually unknown to each other) who hold title as tenants-in-common. The property itself is commonly called a Tenant in Common or TIC property.

Vast amounts of equity have been placed into TICs. In 2002, $356,600,000 of equity went into securities-based TICs, and by 2004, more than $1,719,713,284 of equity was invested—yes, that is more than a Billion dollars. The 2005 figure was $3,229,208 of equity invested, and 2006 showed continued growth at $3,700,000 (source: Omni Consulting & Research). In 2007, due to a slow down in the 1031 equity and investment flips as well as capital market issues, $2,700,000 was invested. While a healthy figure, this was the first time growth retreated.

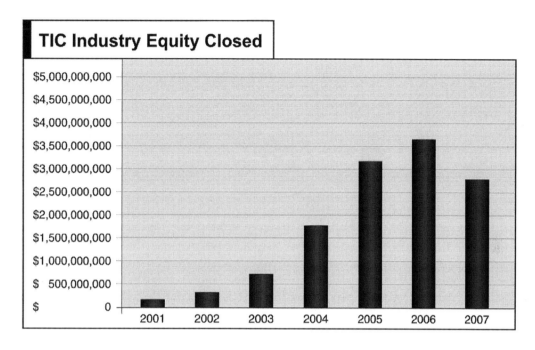

Figure 1. Securitized TIC Industry Equity from 2001 (Courtesy: Omni Consulting & Research). Chart by A3K Design.

Even though tremendous amounts of equity have been placed to date, in many ways TIC properties have seemed to be almost a secret. They are slowly becoming known to investors across the United States. Many of the investors into TICs have been conducting 1031 tax-deferred exchanges, and many of the earlier investors resided on the West Coast of the United States. More and more investors have become aware of this investment type through various channels. Thus, the industry has grown. There are definitely some reasons why we do not see advertising about TICs, including regulatory issues, and yet why so much equity is being placed into these properties.

Why are TICs so popular and why has the industry grown so strongly?

The most profound reason is a 2002 Internal Revenue Service (IRS) Revenue Procedure ruling. This ruling, Rev Proc 2002-22, essentially set forth the guidelines whereby a TIC would be recognized as real estate, not as a partnership. Hence, it could be used in a 1031 tax-deferred exchange. (For those of you not familiar with the 1031 tax-deferred exchange, Chapter Two will go into some detail.) Before 2002, the IRS had viewed TICs as interests in a partnership, thereby disqualifying them as like-kind real property for the exchange.

A small group of companies, mostly in southern California, were offering TIC properties in the 1990s as passive investment choices for their clients. However, since the landmark ruling in 2002, TIC offerings, sponsors, and investors have grown by leaps and bounds. The handful of sponsor companies selling TICs has grown each quarter since 2002. Today, there are more than seventy sponsors. Moreover, it continues to grow.

A second reason why TICs have taken off as an industry is that many investors today want passive income, or effortless cash flow. They want to own real estate, but they do not wish to actively manage property. Many baby boomers may have put more than their share of time in on the "3 Ts"—trash, toilets, and tenants. New investors may not have deep real estate experience. However, they do not want to deal with the "3 Ts" but do want to benefit from real estate ownership. Real estate investors can step into a TIC investment with experienced managers running their investment and gain a cash flow with tax benefits. Some of these investors may be retirees who want something perceived to be more stable or diversified from their other retirement holdings. On the other hand, they may be younger investors who simply want to diversify and enjoy passive income. Many investors, regardless of their age, need to defer the capital gains upon sale of their investment property, which may be quite hefty.

Investors today want to be able to travel or pursue their hobbies and busy professions. They want to have time for their families. They don't wish to manage real estate. However, they like the stability of income and value from real estate. As interest rates have been historically low, interest paid out from money markets, CDs, and other types of such investments have also been low. Real estate income has beaten those returns in the last years and has performed well in general.

Many people became tired of the stock market or at least tired of its volatility. A number of investors decided it was time to diversify outside of paper investments only. In fact, some financial planners suggest that real estate should be part of an investor's portfolio. Some people at retirement age may have seen their retirement funds diminishing at the beginning of this century and onward following record gains in the late 1990s. In fact, starting in 2000, the United States stock market fell dramatically. Over a twelve-month period, the benchmark S&P 500 Index lost one-quarter of its value. Additionally, the NASDAQ Composite Index lost over 60 percent of its value.[1] There have been gains and recovery.

However, because of this, real estate became one of the darlings, if not the favored choice, for many investors. Wall Street also took notice. While everything goes in cycles and real estate will become less popular one day when other investments bring higher yields, many do see real estate as a good choice for diversification and as more 'stable'. It is a bricks-and-mortar structure with intrinsic value on land with value that they can see and feel, and which in many cases appreciates. With TICs, investors gain a number of tenants—often credit tenants—who form the base of the cash flow. While there are risks to real estate, investors receive tangible benefits from their investment, including sheltering of the income they collect each month (unlike many other investments) and the tax deferral at sale if they chose a 1031 tax-deferred exchange.

An investor with $100,000 can purchase $100,000 of stocks, bonds or mutual funds. An investor with $100,000 can purchase $300,000 or more of commercial real estate. Leverage is an advantage in real estate. Leverage is defined as the use of borrowed money to increase your profits in an investment. Building wealth in real estate is usually accomplished or aided by financing. Because more money is invested overall, leverage significantly increases the percentage of profit you can make. Leverage or financing allows you to purchase a much larger investment than you would normally have been able to. Most TIC properties are financed with non-recourse debt, the advantageous kind of debt for investors. Non-recourse financing is a type of loan in which the only remedy available to the lender in the event of the borrower's default is to foreclose on the collateral. The borrower is not personally liable for repayment. In other words, you, the investor, would not

---

1   Courtney Coile and Phillip Levine, National Bureau of Economic Research (NBER), "Do Changes in the Stock Market Affect Retirement Decisions?" *NBER Working Paper 10779*, September 2004.

be responsible for a $60 million dollar loan taken on a TIC property you invest in. Your liability would be limited to the amount of your investment.

There have been historic increases in real estate values in many areas of the United States. Many people have taken this opportunity to cash out on properties that have served them well, perhaps for a retirement nest egg or to build their wealth. I have had clients who realized tremendous capital gains at the sale of their properties, including properties sold in such states as California, Arizona or Florida. By using a 1031 tax-deferred exchange, they could defer paying tax on those gains and increase their net worth through buying or 'trading' into new investment property. With a TIC, they often received better monthly income than they were getting with their former property. (Often rents could not keep up with the appreciation, especially with residential rentals.) Moreover, they gained this new income with absolutely no management.

Yet even investors with moderate gains and/or with enough equity (at least $100,000) to invest in TICs have been favoring the 1031 tax-deferred exchange over taking the cash and paying the capital gains tax. No one should ever have to pay the tax on an investment property if he or she intends to reinvest into more investment property. The 1031 tax-deferred exchange can be a very powerful strategy to preserve capital and/or build wealth, even though one must follow many regulations and restrictions.

The 1031 investor has definitely fueled the real estate investment markets for the last four to six years. Hence, this is another reason why the TIC industry has exploded.

Low interest rates, high property values, gradual economic recovery and lack of confidence in the stock market have all contributed to the booming 1031 market and the TIC popularity.

As mentioned, TIC deals were initiated in the early 1990s by real estate entrepreneurs who wanted to provide property with stable cash flow and no management for their investors. These investors typically had less than $500,000 in cash. Investors with more equity were often purchasing the popular triple-net-lease (NNN) properties if they wanted passive income, even though these are usually single-tenant deals and are usually not institutional-grade.

Some of the sponsors began submitting Private Letter Ruling requests to the IRS in 1998 and 1999, attempting to gain acceptance for their TIC offerings for a 1031 tax-deferred exchange. At that time TIC-structured properties were viewed as partnerships and did not qualify for a 1031. However, the IRS decided it would be better to address the general issues on TICs rather than make a ruling on each deal. So, the IRS took a standstill on all TIC rulings and they finally addressed the issue by releasing Rev Proc 2002-22 in March 2002, which is a procedural guideline for all. Details on this ruling are discussed later.

So, why else are TICs so popular?

Several of the reasons were just addressed. TICs are passive income properties with no management and no daily responsibilities or headaches, which allows more personal freedom. They provide annual income (paid monthly) and partial tax sheltering of that income through depreciation and/or expenses. They can be used in the 1031 tax-deferred exchange. The following are some of the other reasons why TICs are popular.

TICs are easier and faster to acquire than many other types of real estate, which is especially essential for a 1031 tax-deferred exchange. From the day an investor conducting an exchange sells his investment property, he has only forty-five days until he or she must 'identify' properties that he may or will acquire. It is not easy to find, negotiate, study and buy an investment property and arrange financing in these short time frames. In addition, income-producing properties are at a premium and in low supply. There are many potential buyers fighting over a smaller supply. TIC properties are prepackaged and ready for purchase almost immediately.

TICs provide access to institutional-grade properties with low equity. The minimum equity required for purchase may be as low as $100,000 to $300,000, even though this number can be higher and varies from property to property. Usually, with about $100,000 to $300,000, if you wish to leverage into a single ownership property, you would be able to purchase a commercial property in the $300,000 to $950,000 price range, depending on the tenants in place, the type of building, and your credit for a bank loan. Commercial investment properties in that price range usually have local tenants or franchisees of national tenants, depending on your market. These definitely would not be institutional-grade quality properties. They may be management investments as well.

Besides TICs, NNN (triple net) investment properties are the other prevalent no-management income property. These properties have been popular with 1031 investors for years. A NNN property typically has a single tenant such as Burger King, Applebee's, Advance Auto, 7-Eleven, Tire Kingdom, Starbucks, etc. The lease term is usually fifteen or twenty years. Not only does the tenant pay for rent, it also pays for taxes, insurance, and maintenance. The guarantee could be corporate (desirable) or franchisee (less desirable but depends on the size of the franchisee). The typical price range is about $1.2 million to $3.5 million. For higher-rated tenants, such as Walgreen's, CVS, Wal-Mart, Best Buy or Home Depot, the price can easily be $5 million and much higher. Moreover, the cap rates are low for higher rated tenants—at this writing typically 5.8 percent to 6.5 percent unleveraged (in most parts of the country). The investor would probably have to obtain a less desirable recourse loan for acquisition of these NNN properties rather than non-recourse for the single tenant property, except for a highly-rated tenant with corporate guarantee such as Walgreen's. In a recourse loan, you are personally responsible for the loan. Remember, you are not personally responsible for a non-recourse loan. Interest rates and terms are better for non-recourse loans as well.

Most NNN properties are not institutional-grade. Indeed, some investors balk at a single tenant property even if there is no management involved, preferring multi-tenant investments for risk aversion. If that single tenant leaves your building, breaks the lease, or goes out of business, you have no cash flow and will need time to find solutions while continuing to pay debt service. If one tenant among many leaves in a TIC, you might have a reduction of cash flow but all of your 'eggs are not in one basket', like in a NNN property.

You can see that with the same $100,000 to $300,000 and above in equity, you would be able to own a piece of a class A retail shopping center or bank office tower, for instance, that may have nationally known credit tenants in place instead of a single-tenant property. There will be much better financing terms on TIC deals that you could get alone on a NNN deal or most other types of real estate. Unlike the NNN, the TIC property would be ready to purchase, all due diligence would be completed, and all financing would be in place. You simply study the real estate essentials and story on the TIC and the TIC sponsor, get answers to your questions, and then subscribe into the property if it suits you. TIC ownership has truly opened up the world of the institutional grade properties to a large group of investors who would have never been able to buy such properties on their own. This type of property was usually the domain of the pension funds, life insurance companies, or super-wealthy. TICs are appealing because an investor with a relatively small investment can gain ownership to a higher level property.

Some investors ask what institutional-grade properties are. Most in the commercial real estate world use this term even though there is no specific, stated definition and some of the details may vary. However, professionals tend to agree on certain facts when describing institutional-grade, as follows:

Institutional-grade properties are often called trophy properties. They are considered buildings of high standard as well as good design and construction. Their size is also large enough to merit the attention of institutional investors. These buildings are usually located in primary, or perhaps secondary, markets. They are usually in the central business district or a prime demographic location. They may have a name anchor tenant or tenants like a bank or respected Fortune 500 company. Due to the strength of the tenants, the construction, the location, and the street appeal, they are considered to be less risky than other real estate. In the past, the asset classes of office or retail were only considered institutional-grade. However, this has expanded to class A apartment complexes and even some industrial or flex properties.

Now let's return to several more reasons why TIC properties are popular.

Diversification. If they have enough equity, investors can diversify into several asset classes. For instance, with $500,000, an investor could place funds into two different TIC properties. He or she could diversify between types, for example, an office building and apartment complex. He or she could diversify geographically, for example, a property in Phoenix and a property in Atlanta. Different parts of the country experience growth and cycles at different rates. Moreover, asset classes go through their own cycles as well. Diversification is a commonsense approach for investment funds.

Tailoring of the investment. Investment into a TIC or TICs can allow the investor to tailor the amount of the investment to his or her specific needs. If an investor has purchased a single-ownership property but has some funds left over, perhaps $200,000, he or she can use these funds to complete a 1031 tax-deferred exchange (if he or she is in one) and gain additional cash flow. An investor can also be sure to replace the debt (a 1031 requirement) by acquisition of a leveraged TIC property. Almost all TIC properties are leveraged, usually between sixty and seventy percent loan to value. A few will have lower leverage. A few may go higher than seventy percent. Rare is the unleveraged, securitized TIC, even though they do occasionally appear.

While a TIC may not be right for every investor, they have helped supply another option among all real estate choices. They have given the 1031 investor a viable choice, and they have offered another option to the passive income investor.

Disadvantages or Downsides

TIC investments are not risk-free. Liquidity, market and management risks can be considered among the disadvantages. The following list provides a quick, general overview of the disadvantages. Chapter Ten (What Could Go Wrong?) discusses these and other issues.

Cash flow disruption. Your cash flow could be reduced or cut for a time if a tenant or tenants leave and new ones are not engaged, or due to other factors typical in real estate ownership.

Liquidity. TIC properties are not liquid. By nature, real estate is not liquid. You cannot decide that you want to sell today and have the funds available tomorrow. Anyone who is thinking about investing in a TIC needs to know that this is a long-term investment (at least two-and-a-half years to more than ten years). Investors should also go into an investment with the plan to stay until the property resells.

No Developed Secondary Market. At this time, there is no developed secondary market for TICs.

Market risk. If the economy goes soft or the real estate market goes soft for the asset class or geographic location of your TIC, it would possibly take some time to resell the building. The weak market could cause loss of tenants, which ultimately affects cash flow and income.

Financing Risk. Most TICs have non-recourse financing. If the loan comes due and the property has not sold, you would need to refinance. In a rising interest rate climate, there is risk that your cash flow may be reduced because of higher debt service. There could also be difficulty in refinancing. There could also be difficulty in refinancing if, for instance, your building has lost tenants.

Management Risk. Poor management could affect the asset. Your TIC Agreement gives you the right to vote out or change your management company. However, you would normally vote out a manager upon poor performance, and your cash flow may have already been affected.

Capital Call. There is risk of a capital call in a TIC investment, if the reserves were not sufficient and there is need for capital improvement or expense payments, for instance, or due to a loss of tenants. This is not a common occurrence and would usually be a last resort, but there is the risk.

Group risk. Are you willing to be invested with others who are unknown to you in a property? The tenants-in-common will be required to vote on certain key decisions. A good sponsor or manager will lead the process. However, there could be risk of conflict.

Remember, there is risk in every investment out there, not just real estate or TICs. Before investing, you should always contemplate the risks and their impact on you.

The following are a few examples of when NOT to consider a TIC investment:

- If you do not want to lose total management control of a property.
- If the monies for this investment are entirely for living expenses or you have few liquid assets.
- If you cannot make faster decisions than you may be used to in other real estate.
- If do not have or use e-mail.
- If you are not familiar with or comfortable with real estate risk.
- If you need to negotiate everything.
- If you do not really want a passive income property.
- If you are not an accredited investor (this is explained later).

OK, I have a general idea of the advantages and disadvantages. Now give me a brief summary: how does this work? From whom do I buy a TIC property? Where do I find the properties?

TIC sponsors are the companies that find the real estate and buy it or tie it up. They conduct due diligence, obtain the loan, and package it with all necessary legalities and structure. If the TIC is a security (most are), it is sold by licensed registered representatives of securities Broker/Dealers. Most sponsors do not have the proper licensing to directly sell the TIC. The securities Broker/Dealer will approve (or not) the TIC property that has been presented to them by the sponsor before the registered representative can present it to you.

The registered representative will be the professional who advises you of the current offerings and their features. The representative will work with you to understand your financial goals and situation. He or she will help with suitability and assist in reviewing the choices and their details. If the TIC is sold strictly as a real estate-based structure, real estate brokers or agents will bring the TIC to you and advise you of the current offerings. In the time crunch of a 1031, these advisors, either real estate or securities representatives, can be your lifeline to a successful trade and acquisition strategy. TIC properties come and go relatively quickly. They could close in about a month from the time you are reserved or subscribed in the property, depending on the size of the property and the structure. There is a tremendous amount of turnover of TIC properties, and many investors are interested in purchasing.

In the TIC acquisition, your qualified intermediary (QI) will be the third-party entity who holds your funds in trust and assists in specifics regarding the 1031. The registered representative, through their Broker/Dealer, will be responsible for helping you find suitable properties and getting you subscribed. The title company for the sponsor will be involved in the tremendous amounts of closing documents along with the bank and sponsor. Lenders will qualify you for the non-recourse loan. Attorneys will be quite involved in the transactions. Your own team members may also be involved. Chapter Four will go into more detail about the various parties involved and will include tips on what to look for or avoid. Chapters Six and Seven go into detail about the subscription process and getting into a TIC.

Photo 2. Sponsor: TIC Properties, LLC. JC Irving Building, Irving, TX

Chapter 2

The 1031 Tax-Deferred Exchange and TICs

> *The author is not a tax attorney, qualified intermediary or tax expert. This chapter discusses the history and commonly known mechanics of the 1031 tax-deferred exchange. It has been included to help the uninitiated understand what a 1031 tax-deferred exchange is and how it could benefit them. While the author will directly quote IRS publications, she recommends that the readers consult one of the many professionals or publications that specialize in this complex and specific subject if they wish to conduct a tax-deferred exchange.*

Because many 1031 investors find TICs to be a good solution, discussing the 1031 tax-deferred exchange is essential. While many investors across the United States are aware of this powerful strategy, there are still many who are just discovering it.

What is the 1031 tax-deferred exchange, sometimes also known as the Starker exchange, Delayed exchange, Like-kind exchange, or simply 'a 1031'?

It is the sale or disposition of property and the acquisition of 'like-kind' property following the rules and structure of Section 1031 of the Internal Revenue Code (IRC) in order to defer federal tax, capital gain, and depreciation recapture taxes. 'Like-kind' as applied to real estate is essentially any type of investment real estate with a few exceptions such as a personal residence. This means you can sell an office building and buy a retail center or land; you can sell an apartment building and buy an industrial building or hotel.

Educated investors know they never need pay the tax on their capital gains if they intend to reinvest sale funds into more investment property. They also know they can DEFER the tax due by reinvesting the proceeds into another investment property. This is not a tax-free transaction—it is a deferral, which can go on indefinitely and for any number of exchanges, until the day an investor or his or her heirs decide they will cash out and pay the tax. The IRS specifically states in its code:

"No gain or loss shall be recognized on the exchange of property held for productive use in a trade or business or for investment, if such property is exchanged solely for property of like-kind which is to be held either for productive use in a trade or business or for investment."

Section 1031 does not apply to exchanges of inventory, stocks, bonds, notes, other securities or evidence of indebtedness, or most other assets. However, it does apply to some business and personal property, such as planes, boats, or trucks. For purposes of this book, we are discussing real estate to real estate.

A little history to understand the 1031

(Much of this history is taken with permission from the history of 1031 exchanges by Robert L. Sommers; Journal of Taxation, a publication of Warren, Gorham and Lamont.)

Section 1031 of the Internal Revenue Code ("IRC") has a rather long and complicated history dating back to 1921. The first income tax code was adopted in 1918 as part of The Revenue Act of 1918, but it did not provide for any type of tax-deferred exchange. The first tax-deferred exchange was authorized as part of The Revenue Act of 1921 when the United States Congress created Section 2021 of the Internal Revenue Code. Between 1921 and 1970, 1031 exchanges were always simultaneous swaps between two parties. Between 1921 and 1924, they also included non-like-kind properties.

The section number applicable to the tax-deferred exchange was changed from 2021 to Section 112(b)(1) with the passage of The Revenue Act of 1928. The 1954 amendment of the tax Code changed it to Section 1031 of the Internal Revenue Code, and many of our present language and procedural details were adopted.

We can thank the Starker family for the rise of the 'deferred exchange.' In 1979, the *Starker* case gave rise to the so-called "deferred or non-simultaneous exchange". It is an extremely important case for every investor since. The taxpayer, T. J. Starker, transferred timber property which was free and clear of debt to Crown Zellerbach Corporation, in exchange for an unsecured promise by Crown to transfer to him like-kind property chosen during a five-year period. At the end of this five-year period, Mr. Starker would receive any outstanding balance in cash. When the transaction was set up and the property transferred to Crown, a trust agreement was formed whereby the sale proceeds would be held in a separate bank account. The terms of the trust clearly stated that the funds could only be used to purchase the replacement property for the Starker family and for no other purpose. Neither the Starker family nor Crown had access to the funds, except for buying the replacement properties.

When the IRS saw this arrangement, it denied the tax deferral. The IRS argued that a 1031 exchange meant the swap of property between two parties simultaneously. Remember, up to this point, trades were always simultaneous swaps. The job of the IRS is to collect taxes and enforce the regulations, as it understands them. So, the IRS fought against the Starker arrangement. Starker took the case to court. In a monumental decision, the Ninth Circuit Court ruled in favor of the Starker family and against the IRS. The Ninth Circuit found that Section 1031 did not contain the requirement of simultaneity and that an exchange today for like-kind property five years in the future was permissible. The Court also stated that Mr. Starker's possibility of receiving cash in the future did not cause the transaction to fail under Section 1031.

Now, instead of having to find someone with whom to simultaneously swap property (risky at best and quite complicated to accomplish), investors could sell a property today to a buyer and exchange the proceeds into another property from someone else in the future. This was and is a far more practical procedure. However, it also became an administrative nightmare for the IRS. The IRS could see that if property could be sold to one person today and bought from another later, then the application of the law could become not only quite complicated but hard to manage.

So in 1984 and 1986, Congress decided to limit the *Starker* decision with the Deficit Reduction Act of 1984 and The Tax Reform Act of 1986. Essentially, the deferred exchange was codified. Time limitations were defined. Those limitations stipulate that an investor has 45 days from the day of selling his relinquished property to identify property or properties he will buy; he has a total of 180 days to close on one or more of those identified properties. Congress also amended Section 1031(a)(2) of the Internal Revenue Code to disallow exchanges of partnership interests.

The Tax Reform Act of 1986 marks the start of what has become a tremendous explosion in the amount of 1031 tax-deferred exchange transactions seen today. The Tax Reform Act of 1986 eliminated preferential capital gain treatment so that:

- All capital gains were taxed as ordinary income.
- Passive loss and at-risk rules were enacted.
- Accelerated depreciation methods were eliminated and replaced with straight-line depreciation consisting of thirty-nine years for commercial property and twenty-seven-and-a-half years for residential property.

These changes significantly altered the benefits of owning real estate and made the 1031 exchange one of the few tax benefits left for real estate investors.

Eleven years after the Starker decision permitted deferred like-kind exchanges and six years after Congress' actions in response to the Starker decision, the IRS itself finally published proposed regulations intended to answer myriad unresolved issues. Many tax experts say the regulations are relatively clear, brief, well stated and, for the most part, consistent with the body of case law interpreting Section 1031.

Some Revenue Rulings perhaps helped pave the way for the TIC industry. Rev Rul 75-374, 1975-2 C.B. 261 ruled that a two-person co-ownership of an apartment building rented to tenants did not constitute a partnership for tax purposes. The co-owners had hired an agent to manage the apartment property, and the agent collected rents, paid expenses, handled repair and maintenance, and common area maintenance. The ruling concluded that the agent's activities were not sufficiently extensive to deem it a Partnership. In Private Letter Ruling (PLR) 8049064, the IRS ruled that parties to a series of real estate exchanges received undivided interests in an office building and not interests in a partnership. The interests were regulated by a TIC agreement and a Management agreement. PLR 8117040 also ruled that owners of an apartment building were co-owners and not partners because the TIC Agreement provided for majority rule on managing the building, and an agent had been hired to manage the building.

Several early TIC sponsors were asking for Private Letter Rulings to approve their particular offerings for a 1031 tax-deferred exchange. The IRS issued Rev Proc 2000-24, ordering everyone to stop asking for private rulings while it studied the issue of TICs. At last, two years later on March 19, 2002, it made the landmark provisions with Revenue Procedure (Rev Proc) 2002-22. The ruling, which includes fifteen points, provided standards for determining whether TIC interests are considered real estate or partnerships and how they can qualify as like-kind real property for the 1031 tax-deferred exchange. The distinction is essential. Partnerships do not qualify for the tax-deferred exchange. The key point is to avoid the TIC being treated as a partnership and hence being disallowed. Most TIC sponsors provide an attorney opinion letter regarding this ruling in relation to their specific TIC offering.

Rev Proc 2002-22 consists of an introductory section on purpose. Section 2 provides a background, which includes some previous rulings and groundwork for what the IRS was looking for as it made the ruling. Section 3 describes the scope. Sections 4 and 5 indicate the guidelines for submitting a ruling request and what information should be included. Section 6 lays out the conditions that should be satisfied in obtaining a ruling. This includes the fifteen-point guideline. Attorneys usually point out that the fifteen-point ruling is a guideline, not a statement of substantive law. What has developed since Rev Proc 2002-22 is the widespread acceptance of a structure for doing TIC offerings. In fact, until there are any further rulings, most sponsors of TIC properties have adapted their offerings to conform as closely as possible to the fifteen guidelines.

You will rarely see a Private Letter Ruling from the IRS on your specific property. Why? Because the process to obtain the ruling takes a very long time, much longer than what a 1031 tax-deferred exchange would allow. Because the IRS guidelines are clear in Rev Proc 2002-22, the sponsors follow this as closely as possible and obtain attorney opinion letters on the offering.

Rev Proc 2002-22 gave 1031 exchangers a viable solution. In fact, prepackaged TICs solve a problem for many investors. When an investor acquires real estate in an exchange, he or she needs time to find the property, submit a Letter of Intent, and negotiate a purchase contract. It especially takes time to conduct inspections, negotiate loans and gain approval, get permits, licenses, review leases and tenants, review title, survey, and lien holders. All of this is difficult at best, especially if the investor is not already in contract to buy the replacement property at the time of sale of the relinquished property. Here was a ruling that allowed a prepackaged, ready-to-go, institutional-grade property, throwing off passive income, to be purchased in short time frames, whereby all due diligence and loan negotiations have been completed. The time frame to get into this kind of property is well within the forty-five-day identification period. Sometimes an investor may have acquisition complete before the required forty-five-day identification period ends.

The final note about 1031/TIC history regards the Delaware Statutory Trust (DST). Some TIC sponsors offer private placements in the DST structure. DSTs are not TICs. They are passive-income, multi-owner, institutional offerings similar to TICs. The IRS Rev Rul 2004-86 describes a situation whereby the DST is classified as a trust for federal tax purposes. A beneficial interest in the trust qualifies as like-kind property for the 1031 exchange. The DST is covered in Chapter Nine.

So what are the basic rules that I need to know when I conduct a 1031 exchange?

There are very detailed rules that you must follow in a 1031 with no exceptions. All investors should know the general mechanics. If you break one of the rules, the exchange is disallowed, and you will pay the capital gains. When you decide that you are going to sell an investment property, you will want to ascertain that there will be sufficient capital gain involved with that 'relinquished property.' This will help determine whether it makes sense to do a 1031 in the first place—that is, if you were planning to reinvest in more investment property or a 'replacement property.' Your accountant, financial planner, or attorney can help you determine your capital gains if you cannot.

The qualified intermediary (QI) or exchange accommodator is the professional third party who must hold the proceeds of your sale in escrow. You, the investor/seller/exchanger, do not touch the funds—or else you will pay the tax. The QI will handle the specific paperwork necessary for the transfer before you sell your property, assist you with identification of property you will purchase for the exchange, hold the funds in trust, and then transfer the funds for acquisition of your chosen properties, along with other important details.

Find your QI well <u>before</u> you sell your property. Ideally, it should be before you go into contract on the property you will sell. The contract for your relinquished property should contain some specific exchange language. An example of this contract language is:

Buyer is aware that the sale of the subject property is part of an IRC 1031 tax-deferred exchange. Buyer agrees to an assignment of the Seller's interest in this purchase contract to a qualified intermediary to effect the exchange. No additional costs or liabilities will be incurred on the part of the Buyer.

There are many qualified intermediaries and QI companies throughout the United States. Their national association, Federation of Exchange Accommodators (FEA), lists all members on its Web site (www.1031.org). You can also read more about the QI in Chapter Four of this book.

Investors should know that there are no exceptions to the rules for dates and deadlines, even if specific dates fall on a Sunday or holiday. The investor must identify the properties with the QI that he or she may—or will—buy by calendar day 45 from the day the relinquished property sold. The investor must close on one or all of the identified properties no later than calendar day 180 from the day the relinquished property sold. The time limits imposed by the IRS are absolutes. If you are one day or one hour late, your trade is disqualified, and you will pay the tax.

From time to time in recent history, the IRS has granted extensions to exchangers, for example, to those affected by devastating hurricanes. Your QI will know about these rare exceptions.

You have several choices for identification of the properties to acquire. The QI will supply the instructions, and the registered representative or broker can assist:

- **The Three Property Rule**. Identify up to three properties of any value. Acquire one, two, or all three of the properties. Most choose this option. It is wise to use all three slots, even if you intend to acquire only one property. You will have backup options in case something goes awry with the first choice.

- **The 200 Percent Rule**. Identify four or more properties, whose value cannot exceed twice (200 percent) of the relinquished property value. Exceeding the 200 percent limit will disallow your transaction. A few choose this option.

- **The 95 Percent Rule**. Identify any number of properties with an aggregate fair market value exceeding 200 percent of the relinquished properties. Acquire virtually all (at least 95 percent of them, based on the total fair market value). Very few choose this option.

Identifying replacement property is relatively straightforward, and the QI will assist. (He or she usually supplies specific forms to use.) The designation must be made in a written document signed and dated by the exchanger. It must be delivered or transmitted to the QI no later than midnight of day 45. A fax is often preferred because it includes a date and time in the fax receipt document. The IRS regulations state that street addresses or property descriptions that are used must be unambiguous. Identification of a TIC property usually includes:

- Property name
- Property address
- Percentage interest being purchased (if known) or total equity raise
- Loan-to-value (LTV)
- Additional information (for example, the TIC sponsor name)

In a 1031 tax-deferred exchange, you must take title to the new property in exactly the same way you held title in the relinquished property, whether it is you personally or an entity such as a trust, corporation, partnership, or LLC.

When exchanging into the replacement property, you must replace both equity and debt at the same amount or greater, if you wish to defer the capitals gains in full. You do not have to place all of your proceeds into a new property, but whatever you take out will be taxed. You need to replace the same amount of financing or greater. If you do not wish to do so, you are permitted. You will simply have a tax obligation on the difference. If you add new cash out of your pocket, you can reduce the financing. In other words, new cash can replace mortgage boot. (Mortgage boot cannot ever replace cash.)

While there are many rules and regulations involved with a 1031 exchange, the goal of this chapter is to provide the basic understanding of the concepts. Consult one of the professionals who specialize in the 1031 tax-deferred exchange for full details, especially relating to your specific situation. The full IRS code can be found on the IRS Web site at www.irs.gov.

Frequently Asked Questions about the 1031 tax-deferred exchange

Question: Do I have to invest the exact amount of money that I received from the relinquished property?

> **Answer:** To defer capital gains, you must invest the exact amount or more. You must also replace the same amount of debt or more.

Question: Can I keep some of the cash from the sale of the relinquished property but exchange the rest?

> **Answer:** Yes, but you will pay capital gains tax on the amount of cash you take. Make sure to coordinate with the QI or your accountant so that it is done properly.

Question: I recently sold an investment property and have the funds in my money market account. Can I still do a 1031 exchange?

> **Answer:** No, it is too late. The exchange must be set up so that your proceeds are held by the third party in assignment. Those funds are used to purchase your new property. You cannot 'touch' the funds, so to speak.

Question: Can I use 1031 proceeds to pay down a mortgage and defer tax. With the proceeds, could I make improvements to investment real estate I own and defer tax?

> **Answer:** No. Paying down a mortgage is not considered 'like kind' nor is making improvements to a property you already own with one exception concerning construction leasehold exchanges.

Question: What is "boot"?

> **Answer:** "Boot" is anything of value exchanged that is not "like-kind" to the relinquished property. This is usually cash or mortgage debt used to equalize the transaction.

Question: Can I sell one large property and buy several smaller ones?

> **Answer:** Absolutely. Many TIC investors in fact sell one property and diversify into several. An investor may sell many properties and buy one, or sell one and buy many. It is the equity and debt that must be replaced, not the number of properties. However, you must follow the identification rules.

Question: What if the property was held in a Trust or owned by a corporation? What if a Partnership or LLC wants to do a 1031 with investment property they own?

> **Answer:** No problem. The entity in which you sell your relinquished property is the entity in which you must take title.

Question: I've heard that a Special Purpose (or Single Purpose/Single Member) Entity LLC (SPE LLC) will be formed for me in a TIC investment. Won't that disqualify the trade?

> **Answer:** No. The SPE LLC is a disregarded entity (disregarded or invisible for income tax purposes) and is a flow-through entity that serves to protect you from the other investors—like a firewall—and to help reduce liability. The lender usually requires that this entity be used. It does not affect your 1031 exchange or entity regulations. The SPE LLC name is usually the name of the property and a number (South Main LLC 1, South Main LLC 2, etc.), but it could be whatever the attorney deems it should be. Your monthly payments will be made in the name of the entity. The SPE LLC is discussed further in Chapter Six.

Question: Can my own attorney or CPA serve as my QI?

> **Answer:** No. A QI must remain completely independent and cannot have been your agent in the past two years.

Question: Is there a limit to the number of exchanges I can do in a year? I have several properties that I want to sell.

> **Answer:** No. No limit is specified. Just make sure the properties are indeed investment properties that were "acquired and held for productive use in a trade or business."

Question: Is the 1031 tax-deferred exchange only for capital gains?

> **Answer:** No. The 1031 applies to capital gains taxes (15 percent), depreciation recapture (25 percent), and state income taxes (generally 8 to 9 percent, where applicable). Long-term capital gains taxes apply to property held more than one year. Gains from property held less than a year are taxed as ordinary income.

Question: Can any of the expenses for investing be deducted from the 1031 proceeds without incurring any tax consequence?

> **Answer:** Even though the IRS has not published a complete list of qualifying expenses, there are some rulings and case histories. Transaction costs may be deducted if they are paid in connection with an exchange (Letter Ruling 8328011). Brokerage commission can be deducted. Though, in a TIC, you will not be paying real estate brokerage commission for acquisition. However, you will probably pay commission for the property you sell. Direct costs of selling real estate include title insurance, legal fees, notary fees, closing or escrow fees, and recording fees.
>
> Any cost to acquire a loan cannot be deducted, including mortgage points, assumption fees, credit reports, mortgage insurance, and so forth. Other non-exchange expenses

include such things as property taxes, insurance, association fees, and utility charges. Your QI and/or your accountant will help you with these line items.

Question: How will I handle my 1031 at tax time? How will I account for it?

> **Answer:** Among other things, you will use Tax Form 8824, entitled "Like-Kind Exchanges." Your accountant will walk you through this, as he or she handles your returns. The QI can assist. There are also detailed instructions with Form 8824. Make sure to save all information and closing statements because your accountant will need these.

Question: What if I don't identify property by the deadline? What if I can't get into what I identified or decide not to do the 1031 after I have started the process? What happens to my funds held with the QI?

> **Answer:** The right to receive your funds is actually limited. If you did not identify anything by day 45, your funds can then be released after day 45. If you have identified property but were unable to acquire or buy, you will go through a process with your QI before funds can be released. Otherwise, the funds are not available until after the 180-day expiration.

To end this chapter, know that there are different kinds of 1031 exchanges that are less common, including:

- Reverse exchanges (the replacement property is purchased first; then the relinquished property is sold)
- Construction (improvement, leasehold, or build-to-suit) exchanges
- Simultaneous exchanges

A full book could easily be written about the 1031 tax-deferred exchange (many have been!). If you are interested and would like to know more, I recommend you speak with an attorney or a QI. You should also review the many excellent books on the subject.

IRS REV PROC 2002-22 FIFTEEN POINTS

1   Tenancy in Common Ownership. Each of the co-owners must hold title to the Property (either directly or through a disregarded entity) as a tenant in common under local law. Thus, title to the Property as a whole may not be held by an entity recognized under local law.

2   Number of Co-Owners. The number of co-owners must be limited to no more than 35 persons. For this purpose, "person" is defined as in § 7701(a)(1), except that a husband and wife are treated as a single person, and all persons who acquire interests from a co-owner by inheritance are treated as a single person.

3   No Treatment of Co-Ownership as an Entity. The co-ownership may not file a partnership or corporate tax return, conduct business under a common name, execute an agreement identifying any or all of the co-owners as partners, shareholders, or members of a business entity, or otherwise hold itself out as a partnership or other form of business entity (nor may the co-owners hold themselves out as partners, shareholders, or members of a business entity). The Service generally will not issue a ruling under this revenue procedure if the co-owners held interests in the Property through a partnership or corporation immediately prior to the formation of the co-ownership.

4   Co-Ownership Agreement. The co-owners may enter into a limited co-ownership agreement that may run with the land. For example, a co-ownership agreement may provide that a co-owner must offer the co-ownership interest for sale to the other co-owners, the sponsor, or the lessee at fair market value (determined as of the time the partition right is exercised) before exercising any right to partition (see section 6.06 of this revenue procedure for conditions relating to restrictions on alienation); or that certain actions on behalf of the co-ownership require the vote of co-owners holding more than 50 percent of the undivided interests in the Property (see section 6.05 of this revenue procedure for conditions relating to voting).

5 <u>Voting</u>. The co-owners must retain the right to approve the hiring of any manager, the sale or other disposition of the Property, any leases of a portion or all of the Property, or the creation or modification of a blanket lien. Any sale, lease, or re-lease of a portion or all of the Property, any negotiation or renegotiation of indebtedness secured by a blanket lien, the hiring of any manager, or the negotiation of any management contract (or any extension or renewal of such contract) must be by unanimous approval of the co-owners. For all other actions on behalf of the co-ownership, the co-owners may agree to be bound by the vote of those holding more than 50 percent of the undivided interests in the Property. A co-owner who has consented to an action in conformance with this section 6.05 may provide the manager or other person a power of attorney to execute a specific document with respect to that action, but may not provide the manager or other person with a global power of attorney.

6 <u>Restrictions on Alienation</u>. In general, each co-owner must have the rights to transfer, partition, and encumber the co-owner's undivided interest in the Property without the agreement or approval of any person. However, restrictions on the right to transfer, partition, or encumber interests in the Property that are required by a lender and that are consistent with customary commercial lending practices are not prohibited. See section 6.14 of this revenue procedure for restrictions on who may be a lender. Moreover, the co-owners, the sponsor, or the lessee may have a right of first offer (the right to have the first opportunity to offer to purchase the co-ownership interest) with respect to any co-owner's exercise of the right to transfer the co-ownership interest in the Property. In addition, a co-owner may agree to offer the co-ownership interest for sale to the other co-owners, the sponsor, or the lessee at fair market value (determined as of the time the partition right is exercised) before exercising any right to partition.

7 <u>Sharing Proceeds and Liabilities upon Sale of Property</u>. If the Property is sold, any debt secured by a blanket lien must be satisfied and the remaining sales proceeds must be distributed to the co-owners.

8   Proportionate Sharing of Profits and Losses. Each co-owner must share in all revenues generated by the Property and all costs associated with the Property in proportion to the co-owner's undivided interest in the Property. Neither the other co-owners, nor the sponsor, nor the manager may advance funds to a co-owner to meet expenses associated with the co-ownership interest, unless the advance is recourse to the co-owner (and, where the co-owner is a disregarded entity, the owner of the co-owner) and is not for a period exceeding 31 days.

9   Proportionate Sharing of Debt. The co-owners must share in any indebtedness secured by a blanket lien in proportion to their undivided interests.

10 Options. A co-owner may issue an option to purchase the co-owner's undivided interest (call option), provided that the exercise price for the call option reflects the fair market value of the Property determined as of the time the option is exercised. For this purpose, the fair market value of an undivided interest in the Property is equal to the co-owner's percentage interest in the Property multiplied by the fair market value of the Property as a whole. A co-owner may not acquire an option to sell the co-owner's undivided interest (put option) to the sponsor, the lessee, another co-owner, or the lender, or any person related to the sponsor, the lessee, another co-owner, or the lender.

11 No Business Activities. The co-owners' activities must be limited to those customarily performed in connection with the maintenance and repair of rental real property (customary activities). See Rev. Rul. 75-374, 1975-2 C.B. 261. Activities will be treated as customary activities for this purpose if the activities would not prevent an amount received by an organization described in § 511(a)(2) from qualifying as rent under § 512(b)(3)(A) and the regulations thereunder. In determining the co-owners' activities, all activities of the co-owners, their agents, and any persons related to the co-owners with respect to the Property will be taken into account, whether or not those activities are performed by the co-owners in their capacities as co-owners. For example, if the sponsor or a lessee is a co-owner, then all of the activities of the sponsor or lessee (or any person related to the sponsor or lessee) with respect to the Property will be taken into account in determining whether the co-owners' activities are customary activities. However, activities of a co-owner or a related person with respect to the Property (other than in the co-owner's capacity as a co-owner) will not be taken into account if the co-owner owns an undivided interest in the Property for less than 6 months.

12 <u>Management and Brokerage Agreements</u>. The co-owners may enter into management or brokerage agreements, which must be renewable no less frequently than annually, with an agent, who may be the sponsor or a co-owner (or any person related to the sponsor or a co-owner), but who may not be a lessee. The management agreement may authorize the manager to maintain a common bank account for the collection and deposit of rents and to offset expenses associated with the Property against any revenues before disbursing each co-owner's share of net revenues. In all events, however, the manager must disburse to the co-owners their shares of net revenues within 3 months from the date of receipt of those revenues. The management agreement may also authorize the manager to prepare statements for the co-owners showing their shares of revenue and costs from the Property. In addition, the management agreement may authorize the manager to obtain or modify insurance on the Property, and to negotiate modifications of the terms of any lease or any indebtedness encumbering the Property, subject to the approval of the co-owners. (See section 6.05 of this revenue procedure for conditions relating to the approval of lease and debt modifications.) The determination of any fees paid by the co-ownership to the manager must not depend in whole or in part on the income or profits derived by any person from the Property and may not exceed the fair market value of the manager's services. Any fee paid by the co-ownership to a broker must be comparable to fees paid by unrelated parties to brokers for similar services.

13 <u>Leasing Agreements</u>. All leasing arrangements must be bona fide leases for federal tax purposes. Rents paid by a lessee must reflect the fair market value for the use of the Property. The determination of the amount of the rent must not depend, in whole or in part, on the income or profits derived by any person from the Property leased (other than an amount based on a fixed percentage or percentages of receipts or sales). See section 856(d)(2)(A) and the regulations thereunder. Thus, for example, the amount of rent paid by a lessee may not be based on a percentage of net income from the Property, cash flow, increases in equity, or similar arrangements.

14 <u>Loan Agreements</u>. The lender with respect to any debt that encumbers the Property or with respect to any debt incurred to acquire an undivided interest in the Property may not be a related person to any co-owner, the sponsor, the manager, or any lessee of the Property.

15 <u>Payments to Sponsor</u>. Except as otherwise provided in this revenue procedure, the amount of any payment to the sponsor for the acquisition of the co-ownership interest (and the amount of any fees paid to the sponsor for services) must reflect the fair market value of the acquired co-ownership interest (or the services rendered) and may not depend, in whole or in part, on the income or profits derived by any person from the Property.

Figure 2. Revenue Procedure 2002-22.

Photos 3. Sponsor: Passco Real Estate Enterprises, Inc. Two views of the Howard Hughes Promenade, Los Angeles, CA

Chapter 3

Securities or Real Estate?

Securities or real estate? That is the question!

This question has been hotly debated in the TIC industry since 2002. Are TIC properties real estate? Are TIC properties a security? Why is there the debate and such controversy? Why would a piece of real estate be considered a security and sold as such?

While TIC properties are indeed brick-and-mortar real estate and were qualified by the IRS as like-kind real estate for the 1031 tax-deferred exchange, another factor comes into play, specifically the *Howey* Decision, or Howey Test. In the *Howey* Decision, the United States Supreme Court determined an investment contract is included in the definition of a security. An investment contract is defined as an investment of money into a common enterprise with the expectation of profits derived primarily from the effort of others. Hence, most view ownership in TIC properties as an investment contract, and the majority of TIC sponsors offer the product as such.

It seems fairly clear. TIC buyers invest their money into a common enterprise (the income-producing TIC property). They invest for a cash flow, to preserve capital and to make a profit. This profit comes from the work of professional management companies, sponsors and asset managers other than themselves. Specifically, it is primarily from the effort of others.

Further, in the *SEC v. Edwards* case, an investment contract was defined as the presence of an investment in a common venture premised on a reasonable expectation of profits derived from the entrepreneurial or managerial efforts of others. There are other rulings and precedents as well.

However, there are companies offering real estate-based TICs. Some of these sponsors have obtained legal opinions from law firms stating that the TIC interests they are selling are interests in real estate, not securities, and/or that they comply with Rev Proc 2002-22. One of the points in this kind of arrangement is that the sponsor cannot remain in the deal as a sponsor or manager. In the *SEC v. Life Partners* (1996) it was stated that if there are no efforts after the sale, the need for securities law protection is diminished.

The securities side of the industry would say that a sponsor would usually want to stay connected and involved in the deal, not just as a tenants-in-common, and that many of the investors may prefer that they stay on as well. The real estate side may answer that it is a selling principal or facilitator more than a sponsor. Some on the real estate side say they believe some of the real estate TIC deals out there are actually securities and aren't structured correctly, and they must bend over backwards to make sure they are doing everything right to not be a security.

There are certainly some dichotomies:

- The IRS defines TICs as real estate as far as the 1031 tax-deferred exchange is concerned. (However, it defers to an individual state's definitions of real estate.)

- The Security and Exchange Commission (SEC) believes TICs are securities and only securities-licensed individuals may offer to sell TICs and receive compensation for such. It states that TICs and their structure must follow the strict securities rules and regulations.

- The National Association of Realtors (NAR) and some in the real estate world believe that TICs are real estate by nature and should follow the real estate regulations of each state. NAR has stated it is in the consumer's best interest to work with a real estate professional in identifying any real estate investment opportunity, including a securitized TIC interest. The NAR has submitted to the SEC an exemptive relief request for realtors to be compensated in a securities transaction, which is now under review.

- The National Association of Securities Dealers (NASD) which is now called FINRA (Financial Industry Regulatory Authority), regulates the securities Broker/Dealers and registered representatives. It has ruled that only securities-licensed individuals may sell securitized TICs and receive any type of referral fee. In other words, real estate agents or others who are not securities-licensed may neither offer nor advise on securitized TICs, nor are they allowed to receive any referral fee or commission from a securities-licensed individual. (*Notice to Members 05-18,* issued March 2005).

- Real estate-based sponsors believe that TICs are real estate or that their offerings are compliant with the IRS ruling Rev Proc 2002-22, and in some cases they have attorney opinion letters that concur. They pay real estate brokers, not securities brokers or other non-real estate-licensed individuals for these sales. The subscription process is certainly less arduous than for a securities deal, but some question the amount of disclosure or protection for the investor, especially with less experienced real estate sponsors.

Utah legislature passed SB64 in March 2005 that modified the Utah Uniform Securities Act and Real Estate provisions, which exempts TIC transactions from the definition of a security and exempts real estate agents from needing to be securities licensed to receive compensation in that state.

The classification of the deal as a security or real estate does **NOT** affect the way investors are taxed or receive revenues. It also does **NOT** affect their 1031 tax-deferred exchange (at least at this writing). However, the securities world would argue that securitized deals are safer because it is following the Supreme Court rulings and SEC regulations. Additionally, it is safer because there is more scrutiny and accountability than in real estate deals. The SEC is all about protecting the investor. The real estate world counters that it is trained to understand real estate more than a typical securities representative. The real estate world sometimes says that the fees are lower in its deals.

Indeed, many sponsors may rather have their TIC property defined as real estate if they could due to the incredible amounts of time, money, and focus that are needed for the securitization process. However, TIC sponsors who believe TICs are securities undergo the extra paperwork, regulations, and considerable expense to have their TIC interests qualify. It is no small undertaking.

In order to qualify as a security, the project must comply with the rules and regulations set out and governed by the Securities and Exchange Commission (SEC). The requirements are arduous, expensive and time-consuming. The SEC is very protective of the investor. The organization itself was initially created to protect the investor from fraud and misrepresentation. Congress passed the

Securities Act of 1933 in an era when there was little or no accountability or disclosure required by issuers or sponsors. (This is the period of time after the devastating crash of 1929.) The Securities Act of 1933 created the SEC in order to enforce laws and protect investors from unscrupulous behavior. Not only are securities laws designed for disclosure, they also emphasize suitability. Because real estate investments have risks and it is possible for investors to lose their money, the SEC wants to ensure that participants in these transactions have financial substance and a certain sophistication to understand the risks.

For securities-based TICs and other private placement offerings, one form of protection is to allow only accredited investors to participate, as stipulated in Regulation D of the 1933 Securities Act, or stipulate that only accredited investors will be allowed in their offerings. The accredited investor has the experience and sophistication to understand the offerings and its risks that the SEC is concerned about. (Chapter Five discusses this subject.) Some of the real estate offerings require that the investor be accredited, but some do not. Some have structured their offerings much like the securities deals, but some have not. Certainly, there are no requirements or regulations about full disclosure in the real estate world. It operates on the theory of "caveat emptor" (buyer beware).

The TIC securities industry has been very proactive. Its professional organization, Tenant in Common Association (TICA), was formed early on and brings together everyone involved in the TIC industry. The membership has grown dramatically each year. It holds highly attended conferences biannually; members have met and continue to meet with regulatory bodies; and they have subcommittees hard at work.

In a collaborative effort between securitized sponsors, broker/dealers, attorneys and third-party TIC Due Diligence professionals, groups met a number of times in 2005 through TICA to develop what it called *The Best Practices Memo*, which was presented at a fall 2005 TICA conference. The final twelve point memo was presented at the March 2006 TICA conference and addresses the best practices within the framework of applicable securities regulations and industry practices. It is meant to be a proactive approach to high standards, as everyone wants the TIC industry to be a long-standing, successful one for all. This document is still a work-in-progress.

Among the twelve key points of the Best Practices are:
- PPM disclosure enhancements (reserves, tenant lease disclosures, tax issues)

- A simplification and standardization of presentation on costs and loads
- Issues on general solicitation
- Clarification on due diligence (that is, what should be included in the due diligence studies sent to Broker/Dealers for approval and so forth)
- Timing flow of materials (including evaluation, contemplation, and cooling off periods for investors)
- Post-closing issues

In 2005, The TICA ethics subcommittee also published the *Code of Ethics* for the association, which was presented at the fall 2005 conference.

The author most usually sells TICs as securities, but has sold offerings as real estate (she is licensed for both). In her opinion, the securitized deals can offer more protection to the investor because of the SEC regulations, the oversight of the FINRA and the self-regulation occurring in the securitized industry (TICA, Best Practices, and so on). And the Howey Decision is important. However, if a real estate offering is very strong in its real estate fundamentals and structure, the sponsor is experienced, and there is an attorney opinion letter showing that the offering is structured properly and that it complies with Rev Proc 2002-22, some investors may make the decision to go this way on an offering.

If looking at a real estate-based deal, investors must scrutinize the deal more closely and ask questions about anything that is not clear because full disclosure is not required in that industry, specifically:

- What involvement will the sponsor keep?
- How much experience does the sponsor have?
- Who is the manager, and what is his or her experience?
- What due diligence reports are available for study?

Look at the due diligence reports and verify information. Essentially, the most important issues when deciding on any TIC property lie in several factors, including the real estate fundamentals and strength (tenants, location, reserves & insurance, asset type, demographics, property manager, exit strategy, etc.), the strength of the sponsor (net worth, experience in TICs and experience in real estate), an opinion letter on the structure from an experienced attorney regarding the 1031 compliant structure, the long-term life of the property and its appreciation and how the financing plays into this.

It is then for the investor to decide, unless specific rulings or law change this situation.

Photo 4. Sponsor: Sponsor: Cottonwood Capital. Greenbriar Apartments, Columbia, SC

Chapter 4

The Players in the TIC World

This chapter addresses the various professionals involved in the TIC transaction and a description of how they are involved in these investments. These 'players' include the sponsors, the Broker/Dealers and their registered representatives, the qualified intermediaries, the real estate world, attorneys and escrow agents, lenders and property managers, and the professional associations.

TIC Sponsors

The TIC sponsors, as mentioned previously, are the companies that search, find and negotiate purchase on suitable property and then essentially 'syndicate' it. The word *syndicate* or *syndication* has tainted connotations from the limited partnership days of the 1980s. Today's TICs are not limited or general partnerships. We are referring to one of the dictionary definitions: syndication means a group of individuals or companies together undertaking a project that would not be feasible to pursue alone. It usually refers to underwriting or a private placement. This group of individuals or companies joins for a limited investment purpose. Real estate syndicates create, buy, sell, and operate real estate investments.

TIC sponsors (and/or their team) go through all of the due diligence studies on the property to ensure it is appropriate and suitable for a TIC offering. They negotiate and arrange the non-recourse financing, which is quite complicated and detailed. They arrange the complicated legalities and structure needed in order to sell the property as a Tenant in Common vehicle and as a security. Sponsors are responsible for arranging the property management, overseeing the monthly payments to the TIC investors, providing the required tax documentation for each investor, answering questions and handling investor relations and communications, and coordinating the eventual resale of the entire property for the co-owners. The sponsors sign for the financing (recourse to them, non-recourse to you). If there is a master lease structure, they may also act as the master lessee (or one of their affiliates may do so). Remember, most TIC sponsors offer securitized deals, while a few offer real estate-based properties. The real estate sponsors do not usually take all the same steps mentioned.

Some sponsors buy the property first and control it. Then they handle the securitization process and sales. It is more costly to them, but it is less risky for the investor. A larger number of sponsors tie up the property in a contract, work through the securitization process while placing sizable nonrefundable deposits on the property (after thorough due diligence), handle the TIC sales, and then arrange a simultaneous closing. This could be riskier to the investor if he or she is unable to close in a timely manner or not at all. However, the sponsor would usually not submit the property information to Broker/Dealers for approval unless—or until—it is at an advanced, "no turn back" stage.

The sponsor (and/or their team, including attorneys who specialize in securitized deals and/or a Managing Broker/Dealer) prepares the offering memorandum called the Private Placement Memorandum (PPM). The PPM contains all pertinent information about the property, location, demographics, sales comps, financing, sponsor, and examples of contracts (Tenant in Common Agreement, Management Agreement, etc.). It is a disclosure document and can be easily eighty pages or more. It is the collection of information that helps the investor decide whether or not to invest. This document goes to all interested accredited prospective investors. The real estate marketing information may be quite a bit shorter and less complete.

The sponsors themselves may be a real estate and management firm, a real estate investment trust subsidiary, or an entrepreneurial organization. The sponsor may own and manage a large portfolio of properties. The sponsor may have a very high net worth. Not only should the sponsor have extensive experience in various commercial real estate assets, it will also have specific experience in TIC transactions. This type of sponsor certainly has an edge. Some sponsors, especially the newer ones, may not have extensive holdings or a very high net worth. In this case, you would want to know their track record and experience, especially the Principal members driving the investment and company. Do they themselves have extensive experience, perhaps through another TIC sponsor that they previously worked with? Unlike Broker/Dealers, registered reps, attorneys, accountants, banks and escrow agents, Sponsors are not a professionally regulated group.

The TIC sponsor will make arrangements with the title company (often a nationally-recognized firm like Land America or Chicago Title) to set up the escrow accounts, to handle the deposits, to communicate with the QIs, and to handle or oversee the arduous closing paperwork in concert with the sponsor, lender, and Broker/Dealers. Most sponsors use attorneys, either in-house or from specialized firms, for various aspects of the closing and important documentation, such as the Tenant in Common agreement, the Management Agreement, the Purchase Contract, and lender paperwork. Most TIC offering memorandums will include an attorney opinion letter, addressing the structure of the TIC in relation to Rev Proc 2002-22 and the 1031 tax-deferred exchange. Attorneys are also very involved in the PPM and forming the single-member LLC entities for investors.

The TIC sponsor will bring the property to market privately through Broker/Dealers and their registered representatives as a private placement security for 'sophisticated buyers' (with no advertising allowed if it is a security) or as a real estate-marketed property through real estate agents. Some sponsors will invest in a TIC position in the property, an investor, just like you.

The sponsor should be a factor in your decision to invest. Your ideal sponsor has a deep knowledge of real estate and understands the asset thoroughly from its due diligence and acquisition process. In addition, the sponsor can talk to you about it in a knowledgeable way and answer all questions. The ideal sponsor has TIC experience under its belt. The sponsor knows the pitfalls and has a handle on the process and how to manage it. You want the best asset possible, that is, one that has been studied and reviewed for all of its strengths and weaknesses. You want a smooth acquisition process. You want a smooth-running investment that you don't have to think about except to collect the monthly cash flow check. Your ideal sponsor has a high net worth and financial strength behind it in order to deal with issues and solutions and to run a smooth, high-level operation. Your ideal sponsor has a top team of experts and industry connections. You want excellent legal advice behind the offering. You want the best closing agents. You want the best acquisition team: those who can compete with the few good assets out there and win them. You want the best financing terms available in the market. You want excellent management and employees of the sponsor: those who can communicate clearly and in a timely manner, and who give you the correct answers and impeccable assistance you need. Obviously, you want those who are going to manage your asset to the highest levels, specifically the sponsor, an affiliate, or a company that the sponsor may choose. When it is time to resell, you want the knowledgeable sponsor who can help manage that as well. If any downturn in the market occurs or there is an issue with your asset (for example, a large tenant leaves unexpectedly, a fire, etc.), you want problem-solvers who act quickly and know the best solutions. These are some of the reasons why the sponsor matters.

Most sponsors use a Managing Broker-Dealer, which is discussed subsequently. The Managing Broker-Dealer will be involved in reviewing and/or assisting with the PPM and assisting on the placement, handling the mechanics of sending out the PPMs to interested investors, receiving and processing subscriptions for the sponsor, and ensuring all is compliant. Some Managing B/Ds also offer additional services for marketing and educate investors about the offering, including Webcasts or conference calls. Some help with the property closing.

Securities-licensed Registered Representatives

The individuals who are licensed to offer and sell securities are the registered representatives (also called private placement specialists or direct participation specialists; they may be a financial planner as well). The registered representative is affiliated with or 'hangs his license' with a brokerage firm (Broker/Dealer), who, in turn, is licensed by the SEC and is a member of FINRA. The registered representatives are fingerprinted and undergo a very detailed process, courses, and tests before being licensed and accepted by a Broker/Dealer, and then they undergo training with that firm. They must disclose their financials, other business activities, education, and previous employment. Background checks are conducted. The registered representatives are like independent contractors, in regards to the Broker/Dealer. They usually have their own businesses.

You will work directly with a registered representative. He or she will be on the front lines with you in your acquisition of a TIC property. He or she is similar to a buyer's broker in the real estate world. The registered representative in the securities world must first understand your financial situation and goals. He or she must ascertain that you are an 'accredited' investor and that the TIC properties are suitable for you, the requirement he or she adheres to under the SEC and FINRA rules. The representatives will then educate you on the investments, introduce properties, deliver the PPMs to you, and help you review and analyze the properties and their real estate fundamentals. They will assist you in the detailed subscription process (which is rather involved). They fight for your place in a property (as TICs often fill quickly and are in high demand). They help you with the closing documents and questions. They will interact with your qualified intermediary and help you meet your 1031 deadlines, if you are in an exchange. They are your link to the sponsor, closing agent, and lender or others involved in getting your questions answered and in getting the property closed. Much like a buyer's broker, the registered representative advocates for you. During your holding period, he or she usually stays informed on the asset and helps with any questions or issues.

The best representatives take time to educate you on the pros and cons of these investments and help prepare you for the time crunch of the 1031 tax-deferred exchange. They are your 'go-to' professionals who will help get your acquisition(s) completed in the stressful 1031 time constraints.

Like a buyer's broker, the representative is paid commission only if and when you close on a property. He or she is paid by the sponsor through the Broker/Dealer. Registered representatives for private placements/direct participation offerings must have the Series 22 and Series 63 licenses. Representatives who have the Series 7 are fully covered and may sell private placements and a wide array of products, including stocks, bonds, mutual funds, and so on. Representatives must complete several continuing education classes each year. They must always comply with the many rules and regulations, which their Broker/Dealer oversees.

When deciding to potentially invest in a TIC, you may want to speak with several registered representatives who specialize in this asset. Ask the following questions to gain insight into their experience:

- Do they specialize and concentrate in TICs?
- How much time do they spend with this investment type?
- How long have they been handling TICs? (Remember, the business took off after the 2002 ruling.)
- Are they invested in TICs themselves?
- Are they a member of TICA?

- Do they have commercial real estate experience?

You need to be comfortable with your representative along with his or her knowledge and style. You will work with your representative rather intensively for at least a month. You will have a long-term relationship, so you must have trust. You may check the Broker/Dealer's or representative's background with FINRA (www.finra.com). Choose someone you feel a rapport with. Verify how accessible he or she is. Verify if he or she will take the time to educate you, discuss your concerns, listen to you, answer questions, and follow up. Most representatives who specialize in the field have access to most of the same TIC properties. Choose your representative with care. Then intensely concentrate on your work with your representative. For sponsors, it can be quite disconcerting to receive requests for the same PPM for the same client from three or four registered representatives. If you are dealing with several, it can become quite confusing to you and the representatives.

As mentioned, securities-registered representatives are affiliated with a Broker/Dealer. A handful of Broker/Dealers specialize heavily in TICs and private placements. Many representatives who specialize in TICs tend to "hang their license" with one of those firms.

As part of the acquisitions process, the representative will have you complete an account form with this Broker/Dealer because all securities are run through the B/D. He or she will need to show and document that you are an accredited investor and that this is a suitable investment for your overall situation. You may need to complete several mandated forms.

Securities Broker/Dealer (and Managing Broker/Dealers for Sponsors)

The industry-accepted definition of a Broker/Dealer is: any individual or firm in the business of buying and selling securities for itself and others. Broker/Dealers must register with the SEC, and they are members of the FINRA. When acting as a broker, the Broker/Dealer executes orders on behalf of the client. When acting as a dealer, a Broker/Dealer executes trades or investments for his or her firm's own account. Securities bought for the firm's own account may be sold to clients or other firms, or become a part of the firm's holdings.

FINRA defines a member's parent office(s) as responsible for supervising an office or a group of offices. Any main or branch office of a member firm where one or more of the following take place must be supervised:

- Order execution or market making
- Public or private placements
- Holding of customers' funds or securities
- Approval and review of new accounts
- Approval of advertising or sales literature

To be involved in the buying, selling, or trading of securities, a person or firm must be registered with FINRA (Financial Industry Regulatory Authority). FINRA is a self-regulatory organization created by the Securities and Exchange Commission (SEC). Brokers and deals must follow all rules of the regulatory bodies, including the rules of conduct, rules for arbitration and dealings with the public. Broker/Dealer status can be revoked for freely breaking securities rules; for having been expelled or suspended from any self-regulatory organization; for making misleading statements to the regulatory bodies; or for having committed felonies or misdemeanors in the securities industry.

The Broker/Dealer has many roles other than investing or trading, including compliance duties. As mentioned, the registered representatives are like independent contractors with the Broker/Dealers, except the securities world is highly regulated. Hence, the B/D is essential in this regulation and oversight. Also, commissions are run through the B/D on every closed offering. (There will be a split, like in the real estate world, between the B/D and the representative.) By the way, these commissions cannot be shared with non-securities licensed parties, such as realtors or financial planners.

The B/D has an important role in the world of TICs. Sponsors send their TIC offering information and due diligence materials to the B/D, who reviews the materials and decides to approve the property before the registered representatives may offer the property to investors. Not every TIC deal is approved by every Broker/Dealer. If an offering is approved, the Broker/Dealer signs a 'selling agreement' with the sponsor. To give their products the most exposure, sponsors usually sign selling agreements with multiple Broker/Dealers.

In addition to overseeing the registered representatives, handling issues of compliance and myriad administrative details, and signing selling agreements for TICs, some Broker/Dealers also act as 'Managing Broker/Dealers.' That is, they handle the administrative portions of an offering for the TIC sponsor to the other reps and to the public. They essentially act as the point person for the deal. They also oversee and are involved in the PPM and all mechanics of the offering. They sometimes offer the services of marketing along with educational conference calls and sales, if the sponsor prefers or needs these services. Some sponsors concentrate only on the real estate. They are real estate companies and may let the securities professionals handle the other aspects. The Managing Broker dealers are involved by providing basic services to extra services to sell the offering. They are the entity "watching the store," that is, they ensure that the offering is compliant and handled correctly from the NASD perspective.

Financial Industry Regulatory Authority (FINRA), formerly NASD

As mentioned previously, nearly all Broker/Dealers are members of FINRA, a self-regulatory organization authorized by Congress to regulate the activities of securities Broker/Dealers. NASD has long served as a primary private sector regulator and oversees more than fifty-two hundred brokerage firms and more than six hundred sixty thousand registered representatives.

FINRA licenses individuals and admits firms to the industry. It writes rules and governs behavior. It examines these individuals and firms for compliance and disciplines those who fail to comply. It has jurisdiction over its member firms, but it does not have any power to enforce federal securities law on nonmembers, which rests with the SEC and various state agencies.

FINRA issues its Notice to Members (NTM). There have been several such notices regarding TICs. NTM 05-18 entitled *Private Placements of Tenant in Common Interests* addressed such issues as securities law status, application of NASD rules to TIC investments, suitability and due diligence, payment of referral, fees and general solicitations.

Qualified Intermediaries (QIs)

Qualified Intermediaries (QI) are also known as Exchange Accommodators or facilitators. The QI is crucial to a successful 1031 tax-deferred exchange. The QI is the agent who will hold your

1031 exchange funds in trust and assist you in all details of your exchange so it will not be disallowed.

A QI must be an independent party to the exchange transaction. Your QI cannot serve as your tax advisor, attorney, real estate broker or securities broker. He or she cannot be a relative. Violation of this rule could result in the exchange being disallowed by the IRS.

In 1990, the IRS issued Safe Harbor Regulations, which defined the QI rules of conducting business. Shortly after this period, QIs established an association called the Federation of Exchange Accommodators (FEA) to provide some regulation over its members and further its involvement in legislative matters and industry education. FEA also established a certified exchange specialist (CES) designation. CES designees must complete substantial requirements and demonstrate competence in the industry. All FEA members must comply with its code of ethics.

You will engage the services of a QI through a contractual agreement. Your sale proceeds will go directly to the QI at closing and will be held in order to acquire the replacement property. The QI will then deliver the funds directly to the closing agent, who deeds the property directly to you. Without a QI and the contractual exchange agreement, the IRS may not define a transaction as an exchange. The transaction could then become ineligible.

Because the qualified intermediary will be holding your money in trust or escrow, make sure you work with a reputable professional who has experience and is a member of Federation of Exchange Accommodators (FEA). A 1031 tax-deferred exchange can be complicated and stressful. A good accommodator will help you organize what you need to do to be compliant and accomplish your goal. Some of the QI firms are individual local offices. Others are national branches or even Internet firms.

You should look for a company with a track record and experience. Several QI firms were in the news last year for stealing funds. This is an unregulated industry. You may want to consider a bank-related QI since there is some bank regulation. The point is, take care in your choice. A company that has been operating for several years would be important. Always discuss that you will be investing in properties anywhere in the United States. While some accommodators are more local or may not be used to the TIC transaction, others handle them everyday. Similar to the registered representative, work with a QI with whom you have a rapport, one who is available to you and can help you keep dates and forms on track. Make sure one person will be in charge of your trade, not a number of people with no control.

At this writing, the fees for the QI services vary from approximately $500 to more than $2,000. However, the cost can vary geographically. The fees for more complex transactions, such as reverse exchanges, are usually much higher. Some QI's will have very favorable interest-bearing accounts for your funds that can defer the costs and fees of their services. Discuss all fees before signing anything so you know what to expect. Review what services your fee will cover.

Finally, know that there are two other official safe harbors besides a QI for a trade. Rarely would a TIC investor or typical 1031 tax-deferred exchanger use these avenues, which are specifically security agreements or qualified trust accounts.

Real Estate Community

The real estate community is involved in TICs on several different levels. Real estate agents are sometimes the party presenting or representing suitable property to the TIC sponsors for acquisition (and subsequent structuring into TICs). These agents know what kinds of properties are suitable for the TIC structure.

As we know, many of the securitized TIC sponsors are actually real estate companies. Some real estate companies offer a real estate-based (non-securitized) TIC as well.

Real estate agents or brokers may present real estate-based TIC properties to clients. Some securities-licensed agents or brokers also hold a real estate license and may even specialize in commercial real estate.

Attorneys

Attorneys are involved in TIC deals on several levels. Specialized attorneys work with the sponsors, or for the sponsors, on the PPM and the attorney opinion letter concerning a specific offering and its compliancy to Rev Proc 2002-22. Attorneys are involved in the structuring of the TIC deals. They are also involved in the contracts and agreements you will be signing, including the Tenant in Common Agreement, Management Agreement, Purchase Agreement, and so forth. Attorneys are involved on the lender side and with the special purpose entity LLC that will most likely be formed for you in your acquisition. Because the securities world is highly regulated, attorneys are needed to assure correctness in the many aspects of the TIC deal.

The attorney legal opinion will have one of three opinion levels: "Will," "Should," or "More Likely Than Not."

Most commonly, we see the "Should" opinion on TIC deals. This opinion refers to the compliancy of Rev Proc 2002-22 and the overall structure of the offering. The classification of the TIC interest, the disregarded entity, information in the PPM, and any specific issues, such as a master lease, will be covered in the opinion. You will want to see which law firm has written the opinion and review the specific assumptions and the Reliance and Section 230 references. The letter will definitely address how this TIC offering is *not* structured as a partnership. A partnership is disqualified as like-kind property for the 1031. Specific reference to the Rev Proc 2002-22 guidelines will be addressed.

Lenders

Several lenders are now comfortable with TICs, whereas this was not exactly the case earlier. The sponsor negotiates the loan with the lender on the TIC property and works out all of the details so that it is set when offered to you and other investors. These loans are non-recourse. Extensive documentation will be involved, all of which will be presented to you for review during the acquisition process. The lenders qualify you; that is, they complete a credit and background check and ensure you are an accredited investor. They may have questions for you during the subscription process. The lenders will complete the financing for the acquisition of your asset, and the debt service is a major expense of your property.

Lenders are important in the TIC acquisition process. Before agreeing to finance, the lender will conduct its own independent due diligence on each TIC offering. A lender does not take a sponsor's word for details on a property. It investigates independently to look for any flaws or issues in order to understand the performance of the cash flow and other financials. It reviews the sponsor, and it essentially conducts full due diligence. Of course, an appraisal, inspection reports, verification of insurance, surveys and other third party reports are part of the financing process. These are all important facets for investors. If the lender's due diligence fails, the property will not be financed or acquired. This is another layer of investor protection.

Title Companies and Closing Agents

The title companies work in concert with the lender and sponsor to handle your escrow deposits and your closing paperwork. They usually communicate with your QI. They coordinate myriad paperwork for investors all over the United States and pull everything together to get the deal closed for you. It sometimes seems like an impossible task.

Federation of Exchange Accommodators (FEA)

The Federation of Exchange Accommodators (FEA) is the only national trade organization formed to represent qualified intermediaries (QIs) or accommodators. The association also has affiliated members, such as legal/tax advisors, real estate brokers, title companies, and those who are directly involved in Section 1031 tax-deferred exchanges in their business. Formed in 1989, the FEA was organized to promote innovations in the industry, to establish and promote ethical standards of conduct for QIs, and to offer education to both the exchange industry and the general public. It has been active in legislative actions at the state and national level. The FEA provides timely input and updates legislation, IRS and Treasury Rulings, and court rulings to its members. It monitors events that could affect the 1031 industry.

Tenant in Common Association (TICA)

This is the active professional organization for the TIC industry. Those from the many fields in the industry come together in this organization. TICA's members include sponsors, Broker/Dealers, registered representatives, attorneys, lenders, title companies, QIs and real estate professionals. This professional organization has expanded each year since its inception (the then FEA President had initially convinced a group of TIC professionals to form an association). TICA is active in government issues, specifically meeting with the IRS, SEC, NASD, and Congress. It is active in educating its members. Two conferences are held each year in the fall and spring. Panel discussions, new issues, debates, round tables and exhibitions by sponsors are all part of the conferences for the industry. Subcommittees of TICA are also active in various areas such as ethics, liquidity and exit strategy, marketing, legislative, finance, and compliance. Several white papers have been issued by TICA including *Tax and Economic Analysis of Tenant-In-Common Interests and Treatment of Tenancy-In-Common Interests as Securities.*

TICA wants to show the public and official regulators that it is taking action and responsibility for its industry. TICA also wants to show it is self-regulating, compliant and proactive. While this organization includes real estate professionals, it is safe to say that TICA is securities-oriented and is a larger part of the membership is from the securitized world. TICA's Web site is www.ticassoc.org.

Another TIC player is **Real Estate Media**, which publishes a well-written, informative monthly newsletter for the securitized industry entitled *TIC Monthly*. There are industry updates, insider interviews, a sponsor profile each month, information on recent transactions, and other news. The editor, Michelle Napoli, has done a very good job on reporting.

Photo 5. Sponsor: Griffin Capital. 900 Ashwood, Atlanta, GA which was part of a two building portfolio offering.

Chapter 5

Private Placements in Securities
Regulation D Defined

The author is not a securities attorney, securities expert or tax expert. This chapter includes educational information on Regulation D and the Securities Act of 1933 for potential TIC investors. The purpose is to understand the background on the securitized private placements. While the author will directly refer to official publications, she recommends the reader consult one of the many professionals who specialize in this complex, specific subject if he or she wishes to know more. The information, while accurate, is not warranted.

A private placement is a direct offering of a security or securities to a limited number of sophisticated institutional investors, called accredited investors, as defined in the Securities & Exchange Commission (SEC) requirements for a Regulation D offering. In the United States, private offerings are exempt from public registration under the Securities Act of 1933 as stated in Section 3 (b) or 4 (2) of the Securities Act. A private placement is the opposite of a public offering, which would be registered.

To meet the requirement of Regulation D (private placement exemption), the issuer is required to make extensive disclosures regarding the nature, character, and risk factors relating to an offering. The Private Placement Memorandum (PPM), also called the offering memorandum, is the key disclosure document of the private offering. In this case, the private offering is a TIC property.

The PPM is detailed and considered a confidential sales document. It covers the all-important points of the offering, including:

- A description of the offering and its terms
- Risk factors
- Expenses and fees of the transaction
- Cash flow and proformas
- Lease abstracts or summaries
- Information on anchor tenants or tenants
- Details on the construction of the building
- Location and demographics
- A summary of the sponsor's principals and experience

The PPM discloses everything essential, including what the sponsor paid for the property, the sponsor's profit, and the loan terms. The Subscription Agreement and Purchase Agreement (documents used to invest) with instructions about subscribing are included. The Tenant in Common Agreement, Management Agreement, and/or Asset Agreement and other legal documents will be included for your review. These are used to help assess the investment. An attorney opinion letter is usually included as well. The PPM is provided to prospective investors in order to make an informed investment decision. Supporting documents, such as a lease or an appraisal, can be requested once the PPM is reviewed and there is contemplation to invest or the subscription form has been submitted.

During the course of the offering or prior to the closing, it may become necessary to update, correct, or add information, as originally published in the PPM. These changes must be clearly delivered to the investors through an Addendum that describes the changes or additions. Before the closing, the firm must verify that all such amendments have been received by the investors and that the files are accurate and complete.

The PPM can be a little overwhelming when you first receive it. It doesn't look like a marketing piece. It looks like a thesis! Very specific language must be used to follow SEC regulations, including much language about risk. When you first review the information, this can be frightening. However, the SEC and NASD want to ensure you understand that any investment is a risk. Once you have read a few PPMs, you will see that they are structured in much the same way. Thus, it becomes easier to make your way through. No matter how dry, boring, or overwhelming, you should read the entire document. You should then ask any questions you have about the particular investment. The author usually reviews the PPM with a highlighter to mark important issues or questions for the sponsor or to point out pros and cons for the investor.

So what is a Regulation D Offering?

Under the Securities Act of 1933, any offer to sell securities must either be registered with the SEC or meet an exemption. Exemptions have always been available under the Securities Act, but the original exemption provisions, described in sections 3(b) and 4(2) of the Act, were somewhat vague. Therefore, investors or their legal counsel considered them risky. On April 15, 1982, the SEC adopted Regulation D, commonly called Reg D, which set forth objectives and clearly stated rules for exemption. The private placement exemption is based on the theory that sophisticated investors with access to full information about an investment do not need the same protection afforded by registration. If you have a basic understanding of Reg D, you will understand why the PPM is written as it is, why certain rules must be followed, and how your TIC investment fits into all of this.

Reg D consists of six basic rules (Rules 501 to 506). The first three are concerned with definitions, conditions, exemptions, and notification requirements, including the definition of an accredited investor, calculation of the number of investors allowed per offering, and definition of purchaser representative. The last three rules deal with the specifics of raising money. Rule 504 generally pertains to securities sales up to $1 million. Rule 505 generally pertains for offerings up to $5 million. Rule 506 pertains to securities offerings with no limit or any dollar amount, including those offerings less than $5 million. Most TICs follow Rule 506.

The accredited investor definition is quite lengthy, as described in Rule 501. Investors in privately placed securities include insurance companies, mezzanine funds, banks, pension funds, equity funds, trusts, wealthy investors, and you, investors, in TIC properties. Most TIC investors qualify by having a net worth of more than $1 million or a salary of at least $200,000 in the last two most recent years or $300,000 per year if married. However, the full definition is as follows:

Reg. § 230.501.

As used in Regulation D [§§ 230.501-230.508], the following terms shall have the meaning indicated:

(a) *Accredited investor.* "Accredited investor" shall mean any person who comes within any of the following categories, or whom the issuer reasonably believes comes within any of the following categories, at the time of the sale of the securities to that person:

(1) Any bank as defined in section 3(a)(2) of the Act, or any savings and loan association or other institution as defined in section 3(a)(5)(A) of the Act whether acting in its individual or fiduciary capacity; any broker or dealer registered pursuant to section 15 of the Securities Exchange Act of 1934; any insurance company as defined in section 2(13) of the Act; any investment company registered under the Investment Company Act of 1940 or a business development company as defined in section 2(a)(48) of that Act; any Small Business Investment Company licensed by the U.S. Small Business Administration under section 301(c) or (d) of the Small Business Investment Act of 1958; any plan established and maintained by a state, its political subdivisions, or any agency or instrumentality of a state or its political subdivisions, for the benefit of its employees, if such plan has total assets in excess of $5,000,000; any employee benefit plan within the meaning of the Employee Retirement Income Security Act of 1974 if the investment decision is made by a plan fiduciary, as defined in section 3(21) of such Act, which is either a bank, savings and loan association, insurance company, or registered adviser, or if the employee benefit plan has total assets in excess of $5,000,000 or, if a self-directed plan, with investment decisions made solely by persons that are accredited investors;

(2) Any private business development company as defined in section 202(a)(22) of the Investment Advisers Act of 1940;

(3) Any organization described in section 501(c)(3) of the Internal Revenue Code, corporation, business trusts, or partnership, not formed for the specific purpose of acquiring the securities offered, with total assets in excess of $5,000,000;

(4) Any director, executive officer, or general partner of the issuer of the securities being offered or sold, or any director, executive officer, or general partner of a general partner of that issuer;

(5) **Any natural person whose individual net worth, or joint net worth with that person's spouse, at the time of his purchase exceeds $1,000,000;**

(6) **Any natural person who had an individual income in excess of $200,000 in each of the two most recent years or joint income with that person's spouse in excess of $300,000 in each of those years and has a reasonable expectation of reaching the same income level in the current year;**

(7) Any trust, with total assets in excess of $5,000,000, not formed for the specific purpose of acquiring the securities offered, whose purchase is directed by a sophisticated person as described in § 230.506(b)(2)(ii); and

(8) Any entity in which all of the equity owners are accredited investors.

Figure 3. Regulation D, section defining accredited investors.

The following are a few pertinent details of the many in Reg D:

- There can be no general solicitation or advertising to market a specific private placement security. (This is why you never see advertisements about specific offerings or properties that are sold as securities and why you would never receive a cold call.) Only generic ads or educational information can be used. After an offering is completed and sold, a general ad, such as a tombstone ad, or announcement can be made, if desired.

- The sponsor must be available to answer questions by prospective purchasers. All purchasers must have access to meaningful, current information.

- A purchaser must acquire the security for investment, not for the purpose of further distribution or resale. A purchaser must be accredited, but the investment must also be suitable for the purchaser's situation.

- The calculation of purchasers cannot exceed thirty-five investors, unless the lender has stipulated fewer. A husband and wife (or any relatives living at the same principal residence) are counted as one investor.

- Disclosure must be made to the extent that it is material to an understanding of the offering of the issuer, business, or security. If information is not material, it can be omitted.

- Corporations, LLCs, or other entities cannot be formed for the purpose of acquiring the property. In other words, the entity has to already have been formed and already be conducting its own business. (A disregarded LLC entity will most likely be formed for the investor as part of the acquisition, required by the lenders, in which to hold the property. This is different and will be explained in its own chapter.)

- There can be no fee-sharing with non-registered persons such as attorneys, accountants, investment advisors, or real estate agents.

While companies using the Rule 506 exemption do not have to register their securities and usually do not have to file reports with the SEC (most TICs follow Rule 506), they must file what is known as a Form D after they first sell their securities. Form D is a brief notice that includes the names and addresses of the company's owners and stock promoters.

Fees or Loads

According to Rev Proc 2002-22, sponsors must take their profits upfront (*item #15: fees 'may not depend, in whole or in part, on the income or the profits derived by any person from the Property'*). Unlike limited partnerships or other types of group investments in which the General partner or sponsor would take some profit on the backend at sale and perhaps during the investment life, the IRS does not allow this for TICs. The IRS stipulates that these costs must be at fair market value. Costs for due diligence studies, securities fees, commissions, legal, financing expenses, marketing, and other acquisition charges increase the property's overall price.

These fees are known as *load*. Load is essentially the markup the investor pays for a prepackaged investment. Front-end load is defined as the funds paid at the outset of a private placement that do not contribute materially to the actual investment. The NASD limits load to 15 percent. In return for these fees, the investor receives a professionally studied and prepared institutional-grade investment. The sponsor has taken on the responsibility of signing for and negotiating the loan, the cost of due diligence studies, deposits, setting up the legalities and structures, arranging the management, all of the various contracts, and the liability and responsibility for creating this passive income investment.

If you purchased something alone, you would have out-of-pocket costs, and you would spend much more time in acquiring a property. However, load is usually a higher amount with a TIC than in a single-ownership deal. The load will usually create a gap between the acquisition price and appraised price. Of course, increases in rent during the hold period and appreciation will help overcome that gap, but investors should know that load does exist on all TIC deals (even real estate-based deals). In the end, a no-management cash flow and prepackaged property may justify the end result for the investor. That is for the investor to review and decide.

The loads vary from sponsor to sponsor and transaction to transaction. They are disclosed in the PPM. To understand the pricing, though, if there is a 10 percent load on a TIC offering and the sponsor purchased the property at an 8.5 percent cap rate, it would be sold to the TIC investors at an approximate 7.5 percent cap rate. The sponsor lists the fees and explains the items or any special details in the PPM. The industry is working to standardize the fee presentation.

Photo 6. Sponsor: Geneva Exchange, LLC. Honey Creek Corporate I, Milwaukee, WI

Chapter 6

Investing in a TIC: Part One
The PPM
Due Diligence on the Property

The quality of the asset being purchased is absolutely the most important factor. You obviously want to preserve your capital investment, which rests on the quality of the real estate. You want a cash flow, which rests with the tenant quality and structure. You want to avoid problems or a possible capital call. This also rests with the quality of the asset and the strength of the sponsor and/or professional property manager. You want to try to make some money at the sale of the property in future. It is hard to predict, but the quality, management of the asset, and the location will go a long way toward a positive outcome.

The sponsor has done extensive due diligence before purchasing the property. The lender has also conducted its own studies. Before you buy, you need to review the due diligence completed and do any of your own studies. Due diligence is defined as the reasonable investigation performed by a prospective purchaser prior to the final acquisition of a property. This can include studies of the asset, demographics, tenant, financials, the sponsor, etc. The due diligence information is included in the PPM, and certain further information can be provided upon request. For instance, the leases are not usually included page-for-page in the PPM, though an abstract or summary usually is, nor is the building inspection or appraisal. One commercial lease can easily be at least thirty pages or more, and other third party reports can each be as thick as the PPM itself.

Let's start with the PPM.

As you start to review a number of PPMs, you will see that they have much of the same structure. There will always be a similar format for the cover page and language. Sections may include the following:

- Who May Invest
- Risk Factors
- How to Subscribe
- Estimated Use of Proceeds
- Description of the Property
- Acquisition Terms and Financing
- Plan of Distribution
- The Property and Physical Characteristics
- The Tenants
- Demographics and Area Studies
- The Sponsor
- Conflicts of Interest
- Compensation of Sponsor and Property Manager
- Call Option

The PPM will also include a summary of the various agreements, such as Purchase, Management, TIC Agreement, etc. There is usually a section on federal income tax consequences, a legal opinion, and all proformas and projections.

Each PPM will be numbered on the cover page—the sponsor must keep records on which books went to which prospects and a Broker/Dealer form may request the PPM number. The text will immediately define a 1 percent interest in equity and debt for the TIC. The PPM cover page will include the name of the property (the legal name, which is usually an LLC). The required minimum investment is then stated, for instance, a 3 percent interest. The minimum and maximum offering amounts then follow. The maximum offering amount is the total equity that is being raised from investors.

Some PPMs will include definition of an LLC unit and the minimum units required for investment. Don't get confused. An LLC unit is not for a 1031 tax-deferred exchange. This is an all-cash investment into the property, usually at a much smaller investment amount. It may qualify for use of IRA funds. Actually, one tenants-in-common member will be this LLC. The investors will be members of the specific LLC. They will not be on the deed individually; the LLC will be. Not all offerings have LLC investment possibilities. Be clear when reading the subscription procedures for LLC units. They will be different from those for the TIC investment.

Securities-required language will appear on the early pages and throughout the PPM, including such language as "an investment in the interest or units hereby offered is highly speculative and involves substantial investment and tax risks." Language also states that the interests have not been approved or disapproved by the SEC or any regulatory body and cannot be presented as such. Language in the front section also emphasizes that interests are subject to restrictions on transferability. This means that interests are not liquid.

The front section will usually include a small chart showing price to purchasers, selling commissions, and proceeds to the company. There will be detailed information on use of funds and fees in the PPM. For easier comparison between offerings and a better understanding of all fees, members of TICA have proposed that all sponsors use the same language and fee lines. The Estimated Use of Proceeds will usually break down as marked below. (The actual amount (minimum and maximum) as well as the percentage of the overall offering price will be included.)

- **Gross Offering Proceeds:** The equity raised
- **Organization and Offering:** The PPM will state that the manager is entitled to be reimbursed for a certain amount or percentage of expenses in connection with the offering, as this is a securities requirement. This can include printing expenses, opinion letters, accounting, organization of the LLC and structuring fees, E&O insurance, etc. This line item normally ranges from 1 to 3 percent +/-. A Managing Broker/Dealer may be reimbursed for some marketing costs as well.
- **Selling Commissions:** The amount that will be paid to the Broker/Dealers and registered representatives
- **Marketing:** Some combine this with due diligence or other items, and others let it stand alone. Marketing can include payments to a wholesaler for marketing as well as reimbursement for marketing costs, materials, travel and mailing costs.

- **Due Diligence**: This includes fees for the due diligence studies, third-party reports, and work associated with the acquisition studies. Securities regulations provide for reimbursement due to the critical nature of the PPM and the disclosure requirements.

The preceding fees are required to be taken up front in the security offerings. There will be a line following these items, which is "Available for Investment." This is the gross equity raise less the preceding fees.

- **Down Payment**: The amount of equity that will be placed down

- **Sponsor Compensation**: You may see this as a line item. Some sponsors receive a commission or fee for acquiring the property. Some include this item in the use of proceeds while others will disclose the commission or their compensation elsewhere, perhaps as a commission they have received in buying the property, the management or asset management fee, or other.

- **Proceeds to Fund the Loan Reserves:** The lender often requires some reserves to be funded at Closing. These are the investor's monies, but they are held in trust for future potential use, such as capital improvements or releasing build-outs and fees. It is important to fund reserves to avoid potential capital calls and to properly care for the asset. Any unused reserves are refunded to investors at the time of the sale.

- **Loan Fee and Legal Lender Fees:** This will include whatever the lender is collecting for its services and/or for any mortgage broker who may have helped procure the loan. It may include the fees for credit checks, background checks, SPE LLC formation, and any carrying costs.

- **Closing Costs:** This is sometimes found within the loan fee line or a sponsor compensation line. It is for title insurance costs, closing documentation prep, recording fees, legal fees, escrow fees, and the like. Some sponsors will stipulate a certain percentage of the gross, such as 1 to 3 percent, for this line item. Others will estimate the amount.

- **Proceeds Utilized:** The amount of proceeds (out of 100 percent) utilized

- **Offering and Organization Expenses:** These are the expenses for the offering outside of the reimbursement required to be taken by the sponsor. This is why you will see this item listed twice. This line may be about 10 to 12 percent of the acquisition. Depending on the deal some sponsor fees are lower, and some are higher.

Another section of the PPM usually describes the Compensation of Sponsor, showing the estimated amount of money the sponsor will—or could—earn.

When you acquire real estate on your own, you will have several out-of-pocket fees that you must pay to acquire or even just study for possible acquisition of a property. These include:

- A new survey
- An appraisal
- A Phase I environmental
- Title insurance
- Building insurance (and perhaps loss of rent insurance)
- Flood or wind insurance, and perhaps terrorism insurance
- Attorneys' fees (review the contract, leases and title)
- Closing costs

If you are going to finance your acquisition, you would interview or meet with banks or a mortgage broker, negotiate a loan, and supply myriad paperwork. You will incur a number of financing fees. No real estate acquisition is without fees and costs. The TIC acquisition does have additional fees, especially because of the legal structure. However, if your goal is a passive income into a higher level institutional-grade investment, this is the price you will pay for a prepackaged deal. Run the net numbers on the property you manage or would manage yourself. Factor in the hours of work and time involved. Review your bottom-line goals. Many find that TICs compare favorably.

Continuing with the PPM, there will be disclosure that subscriptions can be rejected for any or no reason. There will be disclosure that the information contained should not be construed as tax or legal advice. The sponsor recommends that your attorney or accountant give such advice because each investor's situation is different. Sections on general and tax risks as well as conflicts of interest are usually included. The building will be described in detail, including tenants, location, demographics, and financing. Everything about the offering will then follow. The Income and Expense reports, Proformas, estimates on resale, and other charts are usually found near the end of the book. A copy of the attorney opinion letter as well as copies of all subscription materials and contracts (for example, TIC Agreement, Management Agreement, Purchase Agreement, etc.) will be included for study.

What important facts should you investigate in your own due diligence or compare when choosing or reviewing the PPM on various TIC offerings? You should consider the following subjects. You should feel comfortable asking the sponsor, usually through your registered representative, for deeper answers and for any actual third-party report that you deem important.

Consider if the offering is a conservative property or not. Not all transactions are created equally. Some sponsors may take a more conservative approach while others are more aggressive. The securities Broker/Dealers must decide to approve an offering before it is released to be sold by its representatives. The reality is that most TIC properties are approved by the B/D because most sponsors would not package a property that doesn't seem to make sense and the lender would not approve something that doesn't pass its approval and due diligence.

However, just because a property is approved doesn't mean that it won't develop problems, whether it is conservative or not. Any real estate purchase, whether purchased on your own or in co-ownership as a TIC, could have problems down the road. We cannot foresee the future. We do not know that a long-term tenant may leave early or not renew. We do not know what may happen with the economy in seven years. It is not known today if a storm five years from now could damage the roof. With due diligence, you should look at all of the facts and make decisions based on those facts. At the same time, recognize that there will be unknowns.

You will want to choose the best property for you, based on your goals and expectations. Your goal may be to have a highly rated tenant anchor or have a building with at least twenty tenants to mitigate risk. Your goal may be to buy only in a certain state or to buy a medical office building. Your goal may be focused only on your cash flow income or the potential sales goal at the end of the offering. You may only feel comfortable with a multifamily apartment property while another investor only likes retail. You may only want a master-leased property, while another investor wants a proforma-based offering. You may only want an offering with a very experienced sponsor while another investor is more focused on other issues. There are many choices for your approach to this private placement investment.

Depending on your goals and focus, the following are items you will want to pay attention to. This is not a definitive list, but it does focus on areas of importance:

- Sponsor
- Tenants and tenant structure
- Location and the building itself
- Reserves, financials, and proforma
- Financing (terms, assumable, interest only)
- Attorney opinion letter
- Asset prognostication

The Sponsor

The PPM will include information on the sponsor and principals. Most sponsors also have a Web site with some information, including background, assets managed, and principals. A sponsor may send you brochures about the company. Some of the largest sponsors have been doing TICs even before the 2002 ruling and have long track records that are known. Several sponsors since 2002 have developed good track records and efficient organizations. They may have a healthy balance sheet. Some of the newer sponsors are unknown entities.

Why do we care about the sponsor? This was discussed in a previous chapter. You need a sponsor's expertise to acquire a good property. You need a sponsor's experience with TICs to ensure that everything has been structured properly and the learning curve on client satisfaction is seamless and professional. Many sponsors will have an affiliate company handling the property management. Other times, a top professional local company is hired. In any case, the sponsor will be responsible for keeping in touch with you, making sure payments are made, supplying tax forms you will need, answering questions, and helping to lead the show at time of resale. You will own the property(ies) for some time into the future, during cyclical real estate markets and economic turns. Hence, you will be dealing with the sponsor for some time.

For newer sponsors, the author usually runs a D&B (Dun and Bradstreet) report or other background report. She asks questions that are not addressed in the PPM or ask for more information on the company. Newer sponsors are often prepared for this and have information to provide. I like to get a feel for the principals' experience. A new sponsor may actually have experienced TIC players within the organization who perhaps worked with experienced sponsors previously. A group of well-known attorneys advise the TIC sponsors. If one of these attorneys or firms is working with the new sponsor, it can be a factor adding to the experience level and guidance of the inexperienced player. This is a new, young industry and there will be new sponsors every quarter. It would be unfair to entirely discount a sponsor because it is new, unless that is your strongest criteria in acquisition. You definitely must scrutinize the deal more closely if there is no track record, experience, or net worth.

How a sponsor handles the early stages of the subscription process can be an indication of its organization, as well as how it answers questions and follows up with you. Certainly, a few kinks can occur more easily with a new sponsor. For example, an investor could be confirmed in the deal, and he or she will have to be taken out due to miscalculation. Other kinks could involve not anticipating the time required for getting documents back for closing and the overall, very complex closing process.

Some investors like to meet the sponsor at its place of business and meet the key players in order to understand the sponsor better and gain an overall comfort level.

Tenants

This is a very important area of due diligence. After all, the tenants create the cash flow. Without tenants, you own a building with value but do not gain a cash flow from it.

Many investors like to see a tenant mix in a retail or office property, specifically a mix from different sectors of business. This lessens risk if certain sectors go sour. A tenant mix may also draw a wider array of customers to the building. Lease termination dates are important to review in due diligence. With several tenants, you ideally want staggered dates. If one tenant leaves but you have twenty others in place, you will feel the impact less. A building could sometimes have 80 percent of its leases coming due in the same year, which could be an enormous risk. If you have only a few or perhaps even a single tenant, you ideally want a very long lease in place. You will want to understand the options in the lease for renewal, specifically how much time in advance the tenant must notify the landlord of departure and so forth. Sometimes the sponsor will address this type of issue by approaching a tenant or tenants early and renegotiating a new (longer) lease to address a rollover issue.

You will want to know what type of guarantee each tenant offers, especially a larger anchor tenant on whom you would rely. Is it a corporate guarantee that will continue to pay the rent through the lease term, even if the tenant leaves early? You should know if there are any restrictive clauses. For instance, determine if certain types of tenants are not allowed to lease in the building. This sometimes happens if there is a tenant such as McDonald's on a retail site. McDonald's might stipulate that no other fast-food hamburger business can lease at the retail center.

Some investors like one main anchor tenant if this company is very strong (perhaps S&P rated) and has a longer lease. They feel comfortable with a base of income from a strong company with several smaller, even local, tenants supplementing the income. The anchor tenant lease in retail or even office may be NNN. That is, the tenant is responsible for all taxes, insurance, and maintenance. Some NNN leases are bondable, which can provide an even stronger sense of assurance. For the few single-tenant offerings that may be available, investors usually like to see a bondable lease in place or a highly rated tenant company, such as GE or the federal government.

It is easy to get information on publicly traded companies to review online. The PPM will usually include some information on the tenants. You will want to look at the tenant strength, specifically strength of the business, annual sales, sales growth rates, employee numbers, demand for that type of business, etc. You will also want to look at lease terms, probability of renewing, and the type of industry with its future potential. Every property will have its own tenant story, and each story will have strengths and weaknesses to review. Again, it will be up to you to feel comfortable with the facts.

Sometimes, it is actually better for a building if a tenant leaves. If the rent the tenant is paying is far below market value, you could gain a better cash flow with a new tenant. Alternatively, you could add more diversity at your building with a different tenant. There can be some upside for you in a tenant change. The general vacancy rate of the submarket and area, as well as competition and the general economy for your asset type, can give you an idea on the risks here and how long a vacancy may stand. The property manager will handle the tenants in place and find new tenants.

Some properties may have less of a tenant mix. For instance, an office building by the city courthouse will have a higher number of attorneys and title companies. In this case, the investment could be seen as strong because of the demand of that site (as long as the courthouse remains there). The same could be said for a medical center next to a hospital.

We look at different factors for tenancy at apartment properties, specifically:

- What is the type of property?
- Who is the property serving? Is it university students, blue-collar workers, retirees, or upscale young professionals?
- Do the local demographics bear this out?
- Do the projected demographics for the location over the next five years support the demand?
- How much competition is there for the apartment complex (and how many concessions are needed to attract new tenants)?
- Are there other new properties under construction or permits being requested?
- What are the occupancy/vacancy rates of the market and submarket, compared to the target property?
- Are there any nearby major employment centers that support the center (if the tenants are such that will be using an employment center)?
- How is the university enrollment and health if the property is catering to university students?
- Is the property easily assessable?
- What are the historical operating expenses for the property?
- Is there a possibility of a condo conversion in future?
- Is the area one of high growth or is everything moving to a different part of town?
- Who will manage the property? How experienced is that person or company?

Usually, one of three tenant structures is in place for TIC offerings:

1. **A long-term lease with a tenant or tenants (most likely a NNN lease):** This structure requires minimal management. There is potential long-term stability with tenants such as a bank, a grocery or big-box retail anchor, or a Fortune 500 company in place for a long time. There may be an overriding master NNN lease from the sponsor or affiliate covering the

tenant lease. There is usually an overseeing property or asset manager, usually the sponsor or sponsor affiliate.

2. **Multiple tenants under a master lease:** This is more typical for apartment complexes or some multi-tenant commercial properties. The master lessee is often the sponsor or affiliated company, who effectively subleases to the current tenants. The master lessee is 'guaranteeing' the lease. A few sponsors have double guarantees—one from the sponsor and another from the tenant or seller of the property, who perhaps has given a year guarantee on rents. A master lease stabilizes the income and expenses for the investors. Imagine the monthly ups and downs of income and expenses for an apartment complex. Knowing that a 7 percent annual payment will be paid monthly in year one offers a stabilized income for the investor instead of a potential yo-yo effect. However, it is important to understand the strength of the guarantor/guarantee of that master lease, and know that there are some weaknesses to the structure. An on-site property manager, usually a professional company, a sponsor affiliate, or a successful company that was already in place at time of acquisition, is key. There is usually an asset manager on these offerings.

3. **Multiple leases and tenants in place but not under a master lease (a professional company or an affiliate of the sponsor is managing):** This could be called a proforma approach and is the most common. There is still a projected income and operation, but there could be changes in the income, either an increase or decrease. One of the positives from this type of approach is that, when a new tenant comes on board at a higher rent rate, you can benefit instead of being locked into the master lease payment rate. One of the negative realities is that your cash flow could move down with the property if the net moves down and the property performs below the proforma expectations.

When deciding between a master leased and proforma approach, you can't have it both ways. With a master lease, you are stabilized for good or bad. With a proforma, you can benefit with the ups and suffer with the downs, as you would in a single ownership property you managed yourself. A few master lease offerings offer a bonus program, a payment to the tenants-in-common if the performance is high and there is extra cash.

Location, Demographics, and the Building

The old adage of "location, location, location" still applies. The better the location of the real estate, the better tenants one can attract and the better the value or perceived value. The PPM usually provides detail about the location, the market and submarket, sales comparables, growth, and anticipated future growth of the area. Your registered representative may be able to provide further information on the area, if you wish. The sponsors are happy to discuss this and other details with you.

Be aware of the current and past uses of the building and if there are any environmental issues. Occupancy rates of the area, sales comps, and rental comps should be available for the location.

We ideally want a property in a growth area, whereby new construction, new residential properties, and new industries are expanding or growing. This can help with potential appreciation of the property price, and it can help with the assurance of tenants and desirability. On the other hand, with growth areas, new development could eventually occur in another part of town and draw tenants away.

Another ideal situation is a dense demographic area that is completely built out and in demand. Perhaps there is stability, but not new growth. There is usually competition for well-run buildings as well as a lessened chance of a new building being erected in the area to attract away your tenants. The demographics and stability of the area will be a factor.

Many investors want a primary or secondary city location. Many investors want to make sure the actual physical location of their asset is one that gives visibility and desirability today and in future. For example, the TIC property could be on corner location, visible from a major thoroughfare, or located next to another major asset or a major interstate. The location should provide easy access for tenants and customers. While some investors prefer non-tax states, others want to only concentrate in the high growth areas of the Southeast and Southwest. Other do not mind if the location is secondary or even tertiary as long as the tenant and the real estate story make sense.

You will always want to keep the end game in mind. How will this location's future seem to be in five to seven years or longer? How does it stack up now? Are there any known factors that could make it less desirable in the future? Alternatively, are there any known factors that could make it more desirable, such as a new transit line coming in by an apartment property, a new home development near a retail or office center, or a new airport near an industrial center?

Demographics matter on various asset types. If you are purchasing a multifamily property, you may want a medium income area for an asset that is filled with typical apartment dwellers. Some class A multifamily properties cater to upscale young professionals. There are those that handle corporation executives who move frequently. The demographics of the asset's area would be different from the medium income area.

Several sponsors specialize in university apartment housing. This means apartments that are near large universities and cater to undergraduate or graduate students or professors. These assets tend to be rented all year, and they are definitely nicer than the typical dorm. They may include a pool, tennis courts, study and computer rooms, and common rooms. However, there may be more repairs and maintenance in this type of investment, and the reserves should reflect that. A strong on-site management program is more essential as well. You would also want to check statistics on the university or universities that the property serves. Is the enrollment steady or increasing, or are there problems?

Finally, a few multifamily TIC properties have been offered that include retail and office on the ground floor. This could be a good way to diversify inside of one property.

The sponsors usually have checked on development in the area and any permits (or plans) in place to development new complexes, which could be competition for the asset. They will know which buildings are their competition. They will have studies on the demand in the area, the vacancy factor of the submarket, and information on condo conversions, if this has occurred in the submarket.

Traffic counts matter for your location, especially in retail. This is the indication of how busy the area is and how much traffic uses this thoroughfare. (It also tells your chances of capturing clients for the center.) You can review traffic counts of the area and see if your street is the highest, median range, or lowest. If not included in the PPM, ask about this. Your registered representative can also assist. The desired minimum traffic count in medium-sized cities is about 50,000 per day. A busier thoroughfare in a denser demographic in the Southeast or Southwest may be closer to 80,000–to 100,000 per day. A retail center in Los Angeles may have traffic counts of 150,000 to 250,000 or even more per day.

If a grocery anchors the retail center, check the location of other completing grocers, the visibility and ease of access (location) of your center, what retail supports the anchor, and what other retail is immediately nearby. Everyone needs to eat, but consider if the anchor caters to the area's specific demographic. Many grocers are in trouble due to competition from Wal-Mart (Winn Dixie and Albertsons are two to note). Verify the strength, sales, and situation of the tenant. Determine the location in relation to other retailers. Is it a highly retail-intensive area that draws many people? Is it a more isolated location that might run into trouble or be more difficult to refill if the tenant leaves? Is it the desirable retail section of the town? Is there another area where everything is being built and your building may become obsolete?

Demographics for office TICs should reflect upon the types of employees and clients that may be coming to the property. Is the location prime? Is it a main and main location? Is it visible? Is it desirable? What is the competition? What is the vacancy level of the submarket? How are the rents of your building compared to the other comparable office buildings in the market and submarket? These can give indications of the level of difficulty in placing a new tenant into a building, especially if this building has significant expected rollover. Some investors like that the building has rented under market value, so there is an upside.

As far as the building itself goes, certain facts bear review. Everyone certainly likes a new building. New buildings tend to be appealing, include up-to-date building code standards, and require less maintenance. If the TIC building is older, pay attention to the building inspection (you may want to request a copy) and to the sponsor's discussion of the property condition. What are the anticipated (and perhaps unanticipated) capital improvements? Do the reserves reflect handling this? Has the older building been completely or partially renovated? Buildings in large cities will sometimes undergo a total renovation, and that is a positive. What improvements are being made before the purchase is concluded? If this evaluation is off, you may have a capital call on your hands.

How functional is the building? How attractive is it, regardless of its age? Will it be in good form for resale? Has it been maintained well? Pay attention to details on the roof and HVAC units and compressors. These can be the larger ticket items for replacement. Double-check whether the tenant leases include any reimbursements for repairs and maintenance.

Reserves, Financials, and Proforma

These are usually the first pages the author examines when the PPM arrives. (These pages are usually found at the end of the PPM). Details on the income and projections as well as the expense lines are important. Consider the ratio of the expenses to income. It should be in a range of 30 to 40 percent. Are there any red flags? Were vacancy rates included as well as reserves? Does the proforma seem too aggressive or conservative? What cash flow is anticipated? Are there any increases in the rents and cash flow? Income properties are valued on their income (at least, this is one of the most important ways they are valued). Does the income have upside to keep up with the cost of living index and appreciation for resale? How does the debt service factor in? Most sponsors also make projections in the proforma section for resale prices in the exit strategy.

Look at the acquisition price, the loaded price, and the appraised value. There is usually a gap. Determine if this gap is reasonable or not. Consider projected appreciation and lease increases for value.

One of the very important factors to review is the reserves, as has been mentioned several times. Reserves are the monies put aside for future contingencies, such as capital improvements, build-out for new tenants and other expenses to lease up the property, etc. Reserves belong to the tenants-in-common, but they are held in a special bank account or trust fund. They are accounted for to you. The operating report will show a line item for reserves. Some lenders take a certain amount up front at closing to fund the reserves, and there is a usually monthly amount put aside out of the rent income.

A NNN property, whereby the tenant is responsible for all expenses and who may be long-term, would require a different reserve than a multi-tenant office building with several shorter-term leases in place. (Specifically, in this situation, there could be upcoming vacancies or more changeovers.) A newer building would require fewer reserves for capital improvements than an older building that may need a new roof in five years or other improvements due to age. While there may be a sweep of funds into the reserves at closing by the lender, there will usually be reserves set aside monthly from the tenant income. Unused reserves at the time of resale will be credited back to you as part of your profit proceeds.

Because we are dealing with the unknown, there should always be some sort of reserves set aside, regardless of the tenant or kind of building. A good reserve fund can help investors avoid a capital call of monies. It should be considered part of the operating plan to care for your asset.

One sponsor has a program in place whereby a mezzanine loan is negotiated in advance and accessible so the sponsor can lend to the tenants-in-common if the need would occur and the reserves were depleted. Investors have reacted well to this arrangement. One hopes it will never have to be used, but it provides an emergency net.

Financing

Virtually all of the financing on the TIC properties is non-recourse. Non-recourse is defined as a loan whose sole remedy in the event of failure to repay will be to foreclose against the property securing the loan. Investors are not responsible for the full loan. Only their equity invested is at risk. TIC sponsors negotiate these non-recourse loans, and they can get better interest rates and terms that you or I could get when we buy a local asset, often by 100 basis points or more. At this writing, while typical commercial loan interest rates are at 6.85 to 7 percent, the non-recourse interest rates are at 5.6 to 5.85 percent.

Review the loan-to-value. Does this replace the debt for your 1031? Most loans have an interest-only component for two or three years. You might be wary if the interest-only extends for five to ten years. If the interest-only component is for an extended period, ask the sponsor why this approach has been taken. See if the sponsor's strategy fits with yours. If you are not building equity in the property, you will need to catch up or keep up with appreciation. If the property needs to be refinanced (most likely at a higher interest rate), you need to know where that will leave you.

Find out the loan term (usually in the PPM). Many loans have had ten-year terms, but banks have started to shorten these terms, so you may see a five-or seven-year term. This can have a bearing on your exit strategy. Determine if the loan is assumable. This could be a benefit to an eventual buyer when interest rates are higher. It could be a sales point to sweeten the deal. Determine if there are any penalties if you resell the property early. Check to see if there are any— or could be any—mezzanine loans on the asset to get it closed. Find out the strategy and timing of the mezzanine loan.

Why are the loan details important? One thing to consider, among others, is exit strategy. If the loan has a seven-year term and the economy in year seven is such that you are not able to sell the TIC at a profit, you will have to refinance. Interest rates will most likely be higher in seven years. How will this affect your cash flow? In your opinion, does the loan make sense for the asset?

The loan will be one of the largest expenses on the TIC, and it is important to understand its structure.

Attorney Opinion Letter

Most PPMs of securitized TICs will include (or should include) the attorney opinion letter. The reason for the letter is that the particular TIC offering will be (or should be) treated as real property (like-kind) instead of an interest in a partnership to qualify for the 1031 tax-deferred exchange. The legal opinion is usually about six to twelve pages, even though some may be as long as forty pages. The letter will specify how the attorney formulated his or her opinion, specifically which documents were reviewed, which case studies were used, and so forth. The letter will cite sections of the IRS code and revenue procedures or rulings.

Most letters follow similar format and general content. It will indicate that the TIC covenants will not treat its ownership as interest in a partnership and that co-owners will not take any such position with the IRS. The letter lays out which areas the investors must unanimously approve and which areas can be less than unanimous and if the various offering agreements comply materially. Case law may be cited in the letter to support the opinion.

The letter usually explains how an interest in a partnership is defined in order to clarify the position and opinion. It also usually summarizes the fifteen point Rev Proc 2002-22 guidelines. The letter will address the TIC interests as a security. It should cite the state law in which the property is located and how a TIC interest is viewed in that state.

The conclusion will summarize the opinion and offers the TIC property will, should, or more likely than not be treated as real property for the 1031 tax-deferred exchange. (Should opinions are the most common). Some of the attorney firms that specialize in TIC transactions (and who write these letters often) are Hirschler Fleischer, Jenner & Block, Greenberg Traurig, Snyder Kearney, Baker McKenzie, Foley & Lardner, and Luce Forward, among others.

If an attorney opinion letter is not in your PPM, ask the sponsor if one can be provided. (Perhaps it wasn't completed in time for the PPM or will appear in a supplement.) If one is not available and there is no plan to have one, be wary of the offering. In this case, you may want a specialized firm to look at the offering to render an opinion for you, which is expensive. Alternatively, you might want to pass on the offering. Even though the opinions are rather boilerplate and relate to the offering and not to you directly, you will know that a specialized attorney has taken the time to review the structure and documents of the offering. This is ammunition for you and can provide a comfort level.

Some real estate-based offerings may have an opinion letter. On the other hand, the company may have a generic letter or ruling regarding approval of the structure it uses for all deals.

Asset Type Prognostication

We do not know what will happen in the future, but we can look at historical trends and review the report of specialists. Past real estate cycles and data can help us prognosticate.

While the PPM may address future issues, there are several independent sources of information on general trends as well as market reports on certain cities, if the sponsor has not gone into detail. Your registered representative should be able to assist if the sponsor does not have specifics to supply, if this is important to you.

Very general comments on the 'three main food groups' (office, retail, and multifamily) are:

Multifamily apartment properties may have a good chance of upside, depending on its location, of course. Traditionally, as interest rates rise, families are less able to buy that first home. In a rising interest climate, multifamily becomes more valuable to investors and more in demand by tenants. Further, there have been a tremendous amount of condo conversions in many markets. Hence, a lower supply of apartments has been available for rent. Some areas of the country have experienced high growth rates, and apartments are very much in demand. Certainly, displacement by Hurricane Katrina placed demand on multifamily properties in Texas and elsewhere. Finally, in some markets, there was a moratorium on new development for some years, which has created a lower supply and higher demand in multifamily units. Multifamily TICs usually have a lower initial cash return than some other asset types, but they may catch up due to the nature of the tenant increases in rent. The upside in resale could be higher than the potential resale of a typical office or retail center. Apartments have a more aggressive depreciation schedule (and sheltering of your income) than commercial properties, if that is a factor in your tax situation.

Office properties are more dependent on the economy in general along with movements in their particular market. Compared to retail or large anchor tenants, leases tend to be relatively short. For a TIC investment, you may want to find a property that either has several long-term anchors or many tenants. You want to be careful of your market and submarket vacancy rates and demand. In addition, office tenants may want to move to better and newer sites in their market. Tenants that have put considerable amounts of money into the improvements or have specialized equipment or materials may have more compelling reasons to stay for a long-term period. Likewise, a building that served the only courthouse in town will most likely have long-term demand for attorneys, title companies, and others who work with the courthouse. Sometimes, a building is the signature location for a tenant, perhaps a bank. It has a long-term profile there with strong reasons to stay. Try to understand the tenants, especially the anchor or larger tenants, and the reasons why they would want to stay put. Understand the values of the area. Is this a building that should appreciate and stay desirable for resale, tenants and all?

Retail is at the height of its selling power in general, and it has been so for the last several years. Retail centers with excellent, strong tenants and that seem to have a long business life are ideal. Location is very important with retail buildings. Many factors can come into play. You may have an anchor tenant with a twenty-year lease in place. This is good for stability, but consider whether there are any increases in the rent during that period. Some TIC offerings may be portfolios of strip centers of smaller tenants, both national and local, next to such powerhouses as Wal-Mart or Target. (Being next to large centers would be referred to as shadow-anchored.) Others may be retail neighborhood shopping centers or power centers with large big-box retailers as anchors. While investors have favored retail for some time, there are fears that, when cap rates start to really rise, some value could be lost for resale unless the rents are increasing well and the location is very desirable. Retail centers that come to the market right (that is, not at the most expensive prices), that have good or better than average returns in place, and that have strong tenants have the best chance of doing well on resale in general.

For all asset types, look at the appraised value, and compare this to the loaded sales price. Factor in or estimate appreciation to see if the numbers seem too far apart. As we have said several times, in TIC deals, it is common for the all-in price to be higher than the appraisal. Appraisals always look backward at the historical facts and sales comps, not to the future. When you invest, you obviously want to invest in something that makes sense—something that gives you a cash flow now but will also potentially get you a profit at resale. Most sponsors include numbers projecting various potential sales prices in the future and what your rate of return would be. Review the numbers and compare this to other offerings. Remember, these are only projections.

Different areas of the country appreciate at different rates. Look at the incredible appreciation in recent years in California, Nevada, and Florida, to name a few. This probably will not continue at the same high rate, but it is a factor. Most TICs usually anticipate a 10 to 15 percent return on your money at resale conservatively, and perhaps, depending on market factors, up to a higher amount. A few lucky TIC investors experienced higher returns than others on some resale of properties. However, there are absolutely no guarantees!

Visiting the Property

Some investors do fly to the property to visit, whether in a prearranged TIC investor group tour (not very common) or as an individual. Always let the sponsor know that you want to visit the property so arrangements can be made to receive you for a property tour. There are no hard statistics on the number of investors who visit the TIC they will invest in, but the number seems to be quite low. Many investors feel they are buying a security with information that is fully disclosed and complete, along with photos and aerials. They feel everything they need to know is in front of them. Others feel they must see the property, the general area, and "kick the tires."

When visiting the property, do not ever speak with a tenant or employees directly at a property without clearance from the sponsor. Often the tenant(s), or at least the employees at the property, are not aware of the pending sale. This is common sense that most discreet real estate investors know, but there are enough new investors now that it bears mentioning. Lately, more than once, a sponsor has had the unfortunate circumstance of an investor arriving at a property and announcing he was buying it, thus creating chaos or heartache among the tenants who did not yet know of the sale. You do not want to potentially hurt your own investment!

Due Diligence on a Sole Ownership Property (NNN Passive Income) Vs. a TIC Property Acquisition for a 1031

Many investors who have considered or even own NNN single-tenant properties try to decide whether they should buy more NNNs for their next acquisition or buy a TIC. If you want total control of the property without any management, the typical choice has been a NNN investment. A triple-net lease means the tenant will be responsible for all charges and fees surrounding the property, including rent, insurance, taxes, and maintenance. (Some double-net leased properties also exist, in which the landlord/investor is responsible for a few items such as roof and structure, but the tenant is responsible for everything else. The lease is the ruling factor.) These types of properties require minimal management and have been popular with investors for a long time. However, the NNN property supply is relatively low and competitive, and it has been for several years.

Cap rates are historically low. This means the returns are less than they have been and the price per square foot (if you analyze it that way) is higher. For instance, if a property has an annual income of $160,000, you would buy it for $2 million if the cap rate was 8 percent. However, you would have to pay $2,666,666 if the same property had a cap rate of 6 percent. The lower the cap rate, the more expensive the property. A lower cap rate is also an indication of a seller's market. The NNN market uses the cap rate as the market comparison in the way that apartment properties use price per unit as the comparative figure. In the same manner, land uses price per acre or per square foot, and an empty commercial property uses price per square foot as the comparative standard. Cap rates have dropped consistently over the last two years, even though interest rates have started to rise.

Because so many people want no-management properties, it is not uncommon for a new NNN property to have a dozen full price offers on its first days on the market. Until the TIC properties became an alternate choice for no-management properties, the investor would be in the very competitive world of NNN properties. You could easily bid for several weeks on properties to get an accepted letter of intent (LOI). Sellers often favor all-cash deals and aggressive terms, by the way, as it is a Sellers market. Let's say you finally receive an LOI signed on a NNN property. You then commonly have up to ten days to get into contract. Once that contract is signed, hopefully without any negotiation impasses, you then receive the due diligence materials on the property for study, including leases, title, and so forth.

You may have already lost three to four weeks to get to this point, and you have a total of forty-five days to identify a property to purchase. You have to order the building inspection and new survey. (These can easily take a few weeks.) You and/or your attorney would need to study the leases, the tenant financials, the title, and all of the investigative studies to determine whether the purchase should move forward. What if your due diligence studies turn up some problems, for example, weak tenant sales or a title defect? What if you uncover issues you cannot change, for example, weaknesses in the lease or demographic issues? You would then have only another week to find another property to buy. (This is why 1031 buyers often bid on numerous properties at once). What if the property checks out, but the loan is not approved?

Let's say the due diligence studies were satisfactory. You would have completed a building inspection, an out-of-pocket expense. You would normally have paid an attorney to analyze the lease, review the title and survey (and order a new one), and review the Phase I environmental study (or order a new one). If you are financing the deal, you would have been talking to lenders and shopping for the best deal as well as supplying plenty of information on the property and your financials and credit. The lenders would require an appraisal, another out-of-pocket expense, and other reports. There would be financing fees, and you will probably pay a point. You would have out-of-pocket costs, closing costs, and, most likely, out-of-pocket lender fees. Additionally, there will be the time involved.

All of this is fine and part of the territory in acquiring real estate, but, for those who have decided on no-management, especially less-experienced investors, the road has been rough and very stressful to buy or tie up property in the short time frame and conduct proper due diligence for a successful trade. You will need to have the executed LOI on the properties you identify in that 45-day period. It does not matter that you have 180 days total to close. You can only close on a property that you identified in the first 45 days. For some investors, they were not able to get a no-management property and had to either pay capital gains taxes or buy a different type of property (perhaps a local residential rental) at the last moment.

Enter the TIC property choice and the due diligence solution for the 1031 investor. As you know by now, TIC properties are prepackaged and ready for purchase. The prepackaging includes all due diligence studies completed, loans negotiated, and market studies and location analysis done. You, the investor, only need to study the reports and facts on the property and complete necessary credit authorizations and paperwork for the loan and property acquisition. You may—or may not—want to physically visit the property. You don't have to find the various professionals, such as lenders, survey, inspectors, etc. You do not have to order the reports, pay for them, and then study them. The due diligence reports for TICs are done and available upon request at no charge. Finally, the TIC choice can offer the solution of diversification. Instead of trying to find one single ownership property, which probably will not be institutional-grade, with your equity, you could obtain several TICs. The forty-five-day period is more feasible.

The 1031 is still stressful. There is much to navigate in the property acquisition, but TICs have taken some of that stress out of the situation. Acquiring a NNN single-tenant property can definitely be a solution, but you have one tenant versus several tenants in an institutional-grade property with a TIC.

Photo 7. Sponsor: Rainier Capital Management. Baylor Medical Plaza, Garland (Dallas), Texas.

Chapter 7

Investing in a TIC: Part Two
The Subscription Process

You have reviewed various TIC properties, read the PPMs (or marketing brochure, if a real estate offering), conducted your own due diligence, and received answers to your questions. You have decided on a property and are now ready to invest. You will be subscribing to the private placement offering. Most sponsors have very similar subscription forms and process.

Subscription Questionnaire or Purchaser Questionnaire

The subscription questionnaire is a set of questions that gather your personal information, QI information, and bank information. It also verifies your accredited status and confirms how you will take title. If you are taking title in a trust, LLC, partnership, or corporation, copies of your entity papers, including operating agreement and formation documents, will be requested and will accompany the document. Usually, a personal financial statement (PFS) will be requested at this time, along with your last two years of tax returns. (A few sponsors have recently asked for three years of returns.) Other forms that usually accompany the subscription questionnaire will be:

- Credit authorization and release
- Verification of any bankruptcies, pending lawsuits, or legal issues
- PFS (net worth)
- Entity papers

- Broker/Dealer Page (completed by your registered representative)
- QI authorization
- W-9 (request for taxpayer ID number and certification)
- Last two (or three) years of tax returns
- Escrow deposit made out to a title company

The escrow deposit may be refundable for a short time if at all. Once the sponsor starts incurring expenses (for example, credit checks) and forms your SPE LLC, the deposit is not—or probably is not—refundable. (The author is aware of only one sponsor that incurs a non-refundable deposit at this time). The escrow deposit shows your seriousness, and it will usually be your only out-of-pocket cost in the acquisition. The deposit is usually designated for the formation of your SPE LLC and for some closing costs. At this writing, that deposit tends to be between $2,500 and $5,000, though some offerings have required a $10,000 deposit. It could be more or less and will always be clearly described in the PPM and purchase contract. If you wrote a personal check for the deposit, you may be able to stipulate whether this can be refunded to you at closing and replaced with your trade funds that will be wire transferred at closing. Your QI can sometimes wire-transfer the escrow deposit. Otherwise, you will normally write a personal check, which many prefer to do anyway.

Purchase Agreement

All TIC acquisitions include a real estate sales contract, which tends to be rather standard. If you are used to purchasing commercial properties, these contracts hold very few surprises. You will be asked to initial and sign several different areas, acknowledging the escrow deposit policy, arbitration clause, the as-is purchase clause, the liquidated damages provision, how closing costs shall be handled, and termination of the purchase agreement itself. The contract is not negotiable. If you do not agree and do not sign, you do not proceed. Very few items, if any, are negotiable in these prepackaged offerings.

Forwarding the Subscription Packet

Normally, you send all of these forms, tax returns, personal financial statement, signed Purchase Agreement, paperwork, and payment to your registered representative for processing. The representative and his or her Broker/Dealer are required to have a full copy on record for compliance and audits. Your registered representative will make the various necessary copies (for example, entity papers, tax, etc.), review the forms before sending them to the sponsor to look for any mistakes or omissions, sign the Broker/Dealer page, and include a cover letter with additional information. (Sometimes, you may send the subscription materials directly to the sponsor, but your registered representative will clarify what needs to be done.) Your registered representative will usually handle everything by overnight mail.

You will receive notice shortly thereafter, usually through your registered representative, that you are confirmed into the property or not. The pre-closing process will begin. You will want to identify the property with your QI as you near day forty-five, if not before. Either you or your registered representative will forward the subscription materials and details to the QI for his or her records.

Closing and Pre-Closing Documentation

Depending on the offering and its schedule (and how the sponsor has structured their organization), you will receive the loan documents along with other closing documents several weeks to a month later. The loan documents are usually quite extensive and will require signatures and notarization. One signature requirement will be on the 'bad-boy' carve-out section, which details exactly what bad acts would cause you to lose your non-recourse status (see Chapter Eight for an explanation). Read through this section and understand it. Most lenders, title companies, or sponsors will clearly mark where you need to sign or initial, and if you need to notarize. They will include a return overnight envelope for you with clear instructions on deadlines. Most paperwork requires a turnaround of only a few days, perhaps a week. If you use your own attorney to review paperwork, make sure he is available. Line up a notary if you do not already have one. Many local banks have an notary on staff and you can find a notary in the local yellow pages or with your realtor. Check with your own bank for details.

Sometimes, the loan documents will be delivered to you with other closing documents through the title company or sponsor. Sometimes, the lender will send its paperwork directly, and the title company or sponsor will send the other forms separately. The pre-closing and final closing documents will usually include your LLC formation papers, TIC Agreement, Management Agreement, the call or option agreement, closing statement, QI form or release, title insurance documentation, and other closing materials.

Your registered representative will have already handled your customer account form previously—remember, all securities sales are run through a Broker/Dealer and verification of accredited status and suitability is important. The account form contains your personal information, proof of accredited status, your goals and suitability for the investment, and other information. A personal financial statement (PFS) is usually submitted or is part of the form. A driver's license photocopy will be required, as required by the Patriot Act.

In addition to this, many Broker/Dealers have an order ticket or sales form you may have to sign. It will outline the TIC property you are purchasing, confirm the amount of equity you are placing, cite your PPM number, and so forth. Some Broker/Dealers may have you sign off on a section that makes sure you understand that the TIC is an illiquid investment.

Usually, an e-mail goes out on the day of closing from the sponsor or managing Broker/Dealer, informing you of the closed transaction and congratulating you on the acquisition. A full book of all executed documents will normally come to you about a month to six weeks after the closing. This happens once the sale has been recorded, deeds have been produced and recorded, and all documents have been completed and compiled. Some sponsors scan everything onto a disk for easier management and send it to you and the registered representative. The packet or disk will usually include a cover letter explaining when to expect your first check. As with most real estate deals, the first payment is usually six weeks to two months forward.

You may find that your first distribution will be a check. Usually, a wire transfer to your bank account can be set up for all distributions forward. Sometimes, the wire can occur with the first distribution.

TIC Agreement

A copy of the TIC Agreement will be in the PPM for your review. You will receive a copy to sign for closing. This important document lays out your rights of ownership. The agreements are very similar from offering to offering. After defining the property and effective date of the agreement, there will be the recitals (a list of the undivided interest holders to be named in an exhibit) and wording to the effect that the investors are entering into the agreement for an orderly administration of their rights and responsibilities. The nature of the relationship between co-tenants is defined. The agreement emphasizes that this is not a partnership or joint venture.

The manager is named, along with the term of the management agreement (one year). It also provides instructions on how to renew or terminate the agreement. The management agreement is included as an exhibit.

Importantly, the issues of unanimous and majority consent are addressed. Unanimous consent of all tenants-in-common (as laid out in Rev Proc 2002-22) is required for any sale, exchange, lease, or refinancing on the property as well as anything else stipulated in the agreement. The procedure and number of days to approve or disapprove is included. Majority consent items, if any, will be included along with the procedure. Most agreements will stipulate that a tenants-in-common holding 50 percent or more may be required to approve or review such things as the annual budget.

Language that all tenants-in-common agree to perform their duties as necessary will be included, which usually addresses handling and signing documents in a timely manner, adding additional funds if necessary, procedures for sale of the property, and other issues.

Right of First Offer or Refusal is important. If one of the tenants-in-common wishes to sell his or her interest, then the other tenants-in-common must first be allowed to buy or make an offer to buy. This would address the issue of partition, which would be disastrous unless the TIC Agreement gives the other investors a right of first refusal. (Partition is a court action ordering a compulsory sale of real estate owned jointly between two or more owners. A partition action divides the proceeds of a real estate sale among the joint owners rather than physically dividing the real estate into separate undivided interests.) Several agreements include the limitation on the right of partition. First refusal is also important if an investor needs to sell his or her share. The other tenants-in-common should have the first right to enlarge their percentage share before the interest is taken to outside parties for potential acquisition.

A lengthy section about procedures is usually included. Most agreements include a section about the purchase option of a dissenting or defaulting tenant-in-common. This is usually written that, if a certain percentage (it will vary from property to property) have assented by vote on an item that requires a unanimous vote, then the dissenting tenants (those who dissented by vote on the matter) may be bought out at fair market value or other actions as described in the agreement, along with the procedures for doing so.

Issues such as arbitration, bankruptcy, and power of attorney are addressed. Determination of value is often included in the agreement.

The procedures at sale or encumbrance of the property are also described. For instance, most agreements will include the handling of proceeds following the sale of the property. Any loan balances will be paid off first. Any unsecured loans follow next. Proceeds to pay any outstanding costs or expenses will then be made. The remaining proceeds will be paid to each TIC, according to his or her percentage interest.

It is important to read through the TIC Agreement and ask questions on any issue you do not understand. Confer with your attorney, registered representative, or team members so, if you invest in the property, you understand what you may and may not do.

Property Management and/or Asset Management Agreement

These agreements will be the official documents between the investors and the property manager and/or asset manager, as they lay out all terms of service, fees, and important details. The commencement of the agreement, authority of the tenants-in-common are addressed and usually include collection of rents, repairs and maintenance, leasing, capital expenditures, compliance with laws, mortgage payments, service contracts, taxes and insurance, budgets, financial report, accounts, and tenant relations. There may be reimbursable as well as non-reimbursable costs listed. The financial reports will be furnished to all tenants-in-common in the way governed by the agreement, usually quarterly. The manager or asset manager will furnish tax information. The duties and timelines will be included.

The tenants-in-common have the right to audit or examine the books and records, as written in the agreement, along with any procedures for doing so. Security deposits, operating accounts, and related transactions are all described as well as requirements if the agreement is terminated. The property management fee is specified in the agreement. (It is usually about 5 percent of the monthly gross, but it could be as low as 3 percent or as high as 8 percent). There are differences in the management responsibilities depending on the tenants, often reflected in the fee. For instance, a building with one large NNN tenant would require far less management than a property with fifty tenants, most of which are not NNN. A smaller building versus larger building, or a newly constructed property versus an older one would require different attentions. The fee will also be dictated by the local market and customary commissions as well as the negotiations.

When leasing is required, there is usually a leasing commission paid. This is described as well. (It could be about 5 to 7 percent, depending on what is customary in that market and on negotiations). The asset manager fee is usually quite small. If the manager is a real estate company (or the sponsor itself), he or she may have negotiated a real estate commission for the future sale of the property, which will appear in this agreement or the PPM.

There is usually indemnification language in the agreement between the tenants-in-common and manager.

Call Agreement

This document explains the grant of call rights, the exercise of call rights, determination of value and payment, power of attorney, and the general provisions. Alternatively, it may be incorporated into another agreement. The contract is usually about four pages in length and is relatively simple. It will usually explain that TICs will have the right, but not the obligation, to purchase any interests of other investors who fail to pay expenses or do not consent to a sale, lease, refinancing, or other cases as written in the document. It will discuss the defaulting or selling tenants-in-common and if the agent (sponsor) has the right to purchase interests. Normally, it includes a phrase such as "bankruptcy, death, dissolution, liquidation, termination, incapacity, or incompetency of a tenants-in-common investor shall not cause termination of the agreement."

Be sure to read through the document. Discuss it with the sponsor, representative, or your attorney to fully understand it before you sign.

Photos 8. Sponsor: Argus Realty Investors. (Above) Chesapeake Park Plaza, San Diego, California. (Bottom) Pacific Bell, Anaheim Hills, California.

Chapter 8

The Non-Recourse Loan and the SPE LLCs Getting Paid, the Bank Account and LLC

> The author is not an attorney or a professional in the lending field. The basic information in this chapter about the SPE LLC and TIC financing is being relayed for educational purposes. It is not intended to be a detailed treatise on the subject. The information is as current and accurate as possible, but it is not warranted. Investors should review specific legal questions or issues with their attorney and talk to the specific lender or sponsor of the TIC property for more details on the specific loan. (This can be done through the registered representative.)

Most TIC properties have financing, and this financing is almost always non-recourse. A non-recourse loan is the desirable type of loan because you are not personally responsible or liable. It is a type of loan in which the only remedy available to the lender in the event of the borrower's default is to foreclose on the collateral and not to look to the borrowers. A non-recourse loan is all about the building and its tenants as well as the sponsor or party who brings the property to the lender for financing. The actual recourse guarantor of the loan is often the sponsor, a principal(s) of the sponsor, or an entity. If this is not explained in the PPM, ask the sponsor. You should know who the guarantor is on the loan. (You should also know what their assets are.)

Each TIC property will have a specific loan negotiated on the offering. Many loan-to-values fall in the 60% to 65% range, though most recently this has fallen to the 50% range with the capital market issues. Once in a great while, there is the all-cash deal in the securitized world.

The PPM of your chosen TIC will go into detail about the loan, the lender, and its terms. They are usually fixed loans, usually with an interest-only component for the first few years. Amortization is usually thirty years. Sometimes the loans are assumable. This is a plus when considering the exit strategy and resale of the property. Because interest rates will most likely be higher in future, a lower interest loan could be a selling point.

While these are non-recourse loans, there will always be the 'bad-boy' carve-outs, lists of bad acts that, if committed by an investor, cause the investor to lose his or her non-recourse status. The loan would become recourse to the investor committing the act. Bad-boy acts include physically hurting or destroying the property or committing fraud or intentional misrepresentation. The lists of acts have started to become shorter since 2002 because lenders have become more comfortable with TICs and the structure has become more sophisticated. These documents will be sent for review and signature in the closing stages, but you can ask the sponsor about the carve-outs before you invest or during due diligence.

When the TIC industry started to take off in 2002, what initially frightened lenders when they considered financing these investments?

- Dealing with up to thirty-five investors/borrowers from many states and locations per purchase instead of one borrower
- A future personal bankruptcy of one of those investors could spark a problem with the asset, even a foreclosure
- The incredible amounts of paperwork and details needed because of the many borrowers and the legal structure of the asset

However, as lenders have actively worked with sponsors, many have become quite comfortable with the TIC industry and with the issues. The issue of bankruptcy risk has been addressed through the use of a special purpose bankruptcy-remote entity, the single-purpose entity LLC (SPE LLC), also commonly called single-member limited liability entities. Use of these entities has become widespread. It is now well established in TICs and other types of commercial real estate as well. Most lenders who handle multi-state, securitized, and structured financing now require the SPE LLC, which is good for you, the investor. Essentially, the lender segregates the sole asset of the SPE LLC in a way to minimize the undesirable effects of a bankruptcy. It is a form of protection for you and your asset, a kind of firewall around you and between you and each of the investors. It is an effective way to give you liability protection as well. For instance, without the SPE LLC, an unrelated claim against one of the TICs could have allowed a claimant to secure a judgment lien against the entire property. With the SPE LLC, this is not possible.

The lender usually requires specific covenants in the SPE LLC organizational documents, which you will receive as part of the closing process. Covenants include:

- Prohibition against any business activity other than operation of the property and against owning any other property in the SPE LLC

- Prohibition against any merger with another entity or acquisition of any subsidiary

- Separate SPE books and records, among other covenants

SPE LLCs are disregarded entities in most states. (They are invisible for tax purposes and are considered flow-through entities.) Each investor should check with his or her accountant, attorney, or sponsor on the matter. "In most cases, the IRS will recognize the separate identity of an unincorporated entity as long as the owner does NOT control the day-to-day affairs and otherwise deals with the entity in such a way that it is a mere agent or instrumentality of its owner," according to an article in *South Carolina Lawyer*.[2]

Many states have amended their LLC statutes to specifically permit the formation of single-member LLCs. Several TIC sponsors use the Delaware SPE LLC because it is favorable, but you may see other states used. Often, there could be two entities, specifically one in Delaware and one in the state of the property. This will be addressed in the PPM.

As mentioned, the entity is treated for federal tax purposes as if it was a sole proprietorship or division of the organization's owner. The regulations allow an individual or corporation to obtain the limited liability advantage of a corporation, along with the single-level "pass-through" tax advantage of a partnership with the single-member LLC.

Usually, the lender's or sponsor's attorney will form these entities for you and take care of the formalities. You will receive paperwork for your signature and your files. You will be responsible for keeping the LLC up-to-date each year after that. Some sponsors pay the renewal fee and deduct

---

2   *Thomas Stanley, Fred Kingsmore Jr. and William G. Newsome III; 'Finally, Real Tax Simplification*. South Carolina Lawyer (Bar Publication), Sept/Oct 1997. page 20.

it from your monthly distribution. Others have you take care of the paperwork and fee yourself directly. Annual renewal fees are usually between $200 and $600 for most states. (Sometimes, you are registered in two states.) It is essential that the SPE LLC fee be paid and updated each year, for your protection and that of the asset.

To summarize, each TIC investor will usually have a SPE LLC formed for him or her, which will wrap around his buying entity and will normally be a disregarded entity for tax purposes.

Your first distribution payment is often a hard copy check. The sponsor will provide forms for the bank transfer or wire option for further distributions. You sometimes complete bank wire instructions during the subscription or closing process, but some sponsors need to send a hard copy check for the first month anyway. Most TIC purchases are made in the name of your SPE LLC. Usually, your monthly checks or wire will come made out in that name. Hence, you will open a bank account in that name or talk to your bank about a subaccount to your own. Because the LLC is a disregarded, flow-through entity, it could be a subaccount of your own account, but each bank will have its own procedures. In fact, the lender of the TIC may require that a separate bank account be formed.

When you diversify into several TIC properties, you will have several accounts. That is, most TIC structures are such that they are legally separate from each other for protection. At the least, you will have different SPE LLCs for each investment. You will be responsible for their annual renewal, and you will probably have separate bank accounts for each investment.

Photo 9. Sponsor: Cabot Investment Properties, LLC. BBT Building, Winston-Salem, North Carolina.

Chapter 9

The Delaware Statutory Trust (DST)

The author is not an attorney or a specialist in the DST. This chapter was written to inform the readers about the history and basics of the DST. Anyone interested in investing in this type of property should check with his or her attorney and discuss the structure and issues with the sponsor. He or she may want to look into the subject with specialists.

The IRS issued Revenue Ruling 2004-86 regarding use of the Delaware Statutory Trust (DST) for purchase of fractional interests in property and qualification for the 1031 tax-deferred exchange. What is the DST? Why does this matter?

A statutory trust is defined as a trust created and enacted by the effect of a statute, usually temporary in nature, which may bridge or create ownership of property to benefit a certain class of individuals that the statute is designed to protect. Statutory trusts have been recognized in Delaware since 1947. However, the passage of the Delaware Statutory Trust Act in 1988 clarified the statutory recognition of the trust. The act was further amended in September 2002 and renamed the Delaware Statutory Trust Act. This trust act codified Delaware law for use of trusts in business transactions. The DST is defined as an unincorporated association created by a trust instrument for which property is deposited, managed, administered, and operated. A trustee administers the trust and acts for its members or beneficiaries. The rights as well as obligations of those involved, including trustee and beneficiaries, is determined by contract instead of common law.

A DST property is not a TIC property. They are mutually exclusive. Legally, each stands on its own. Both are group ownership structures for passive income properties, prepackaged and usually institutional-grade. DSTs are securitized like most TICs, and some of the same sponsors offer both DST and TIC properties. However, DSTs are truly passive, even more passive than TICs. Why? The trust owns 100 percent of the property and is on the deed. You, the investor, are a member of that trust. Unlike a TIC investment, you will not be on the deed to the property. The trust makes all decisions about the property. Unlike a TIC, you will not make any decisions at all or have any voting rights. Some investors won't mind this. Others won't like it. The beneficiaries' (investors) only right with respect to the trust is to receive distributions. They have no vote or say on anything, whether it be to remove the property manager or whether it be regarding the sale of the property. Obviously, the sponsors who sell properties as a DST communicate with the investors closely and keep them informed and act in a fiduciary role. An investor will have to feel quite comfortable with the sponsor or trustee in the case of the DST investment because that trustee will be acting fully for him or her.

What is good about the DST?

What is good about the structure? Lenders like the DST. Instead of lending to up to thirty-five TIC investors, they lend to one entity, the trust. (Remember, #2 of the 15 point Rev Proc 2002-22 ruling stated that a TIC can have no more than 35 investors). Hence, the lender on a DST does not have to complete credit checks on all investors. It does not have to handle analysis of each buying entity nor gain myriad signatures or produce the loan documents for each investor. (Typical loan documents could be fifty pages per investor.) The lender does not need to form the SPE LLC entity for each investor, and there is no need for the bad-boy recourse carve-outs for each investor in the non-recourse loan. The lender only looks to the sponsor for the carve-outs. These items keep down the fees and cost of the loan, which can be a benefit to you.

The DST is bankruptcy-remote, a positive for the investor. Provisions exist that prevent the bankruptcy creditors of any beneficiary of the trust from reaching the property. This gives the lender and investors a level of security. The DST also shields the beneficiaries from liabilities regarding the property.

The DST is a disregarded entity. You can draw some comparison between it and the SPE LLC used in TIC investments. There is limited liability to the owners of both entities. They are both pass-through entities for tax purposes. They are both bankruptcy-remote.

Because the DST does not fall within the rule of limiting the number of investors to thirty-five, there is more latitude in accepting investors into a property with less equity or more investors per property than with a TIC. This can also be a benefit for an investor with a smaller amount of cash to invest.

What can be bad about the DST?

The IRS ruling named prohibitions on the powers of the trustee. These have come to be known as the 'Seven Deadly Sins'. If the trust commits one of the sins, it will lose its trust status and become an LLC via "the springing LLC" action. In this case, when the property is finally sold, the investors/beneficiaries would no longer be able to conduct a 1031 tax-deferred exchange because the LLC would be viewed as a partnership. Some have explained that the problem could be solved and the LLC could perhaps be converted back to a DST before re-sale, or do the 'swap and drop.' To date, no DST properties have had to dissolve to an LLC, as they are quite new, and there is no precedent. The Seven Deadly Sins are:

1. Once the offering is closed, no future contributions can be made to the DST by new or current beneficiaries.
2. The trustee cannot renegotiate the terms of the existing loan nor can it borrow any new funds from any party.
3. The trustee cannot reinvest the proceeds from the sale of its real estate.
4. The trustee is limited to making capital expenditures to the property except for normal wear and tear maintenance, minor nonstructural capital improvements, and those required by law.
5. Any cash held between distributions can only be invested in short-term debt obligations.
6. All cash, except for necessary reserves, must be distributed on a current basis.
7. The trustee cannot enter into new leases or renegotiate the current leases.

Because of several of these rules, master-leased properties are most appropriate for a DST whereby the tenant or master tenant takes on all operating responsibilities that the trust cannot take on via a long-term NNN lease. The DST could be a called a "do not vary the investment" investment structure.

Some of the Seven Deadly Sins could be of concern to investors. What if the loan has a seven-year term and the property has not been sold in seven years due to the economy and that loan has come due or will need to be refinanced? The DST does not allow refinancing or new loans. What if a major capital expenditure is needed? This would be something more than normal wear and tear, something unexpected, and something more than what insurance could handle. The DST does not allow this to occur. What if a beneficiary needs to exit the property before resale? One of the sins is that no new monies by current or future investors can be added. What if a tenant goes bankrupt and leaves the property? The DST does not allow for new leases. Potential investors should consider the Seven Deadly Sins, talk to the offering sponsor about any concerns, and see how they are addressed and what solutions exist. Then discuss the risks with an attorney, CPA, and representative.

One sponsor that frequently offers DST products handles the resale issue through a buyback option. Exercising the buyback option could offer a solution before the trust would commit several of the sins.

While there can be some instances where a DST can work and some advantages (for example, less fees, smaller equity possible, more investors per property, truly passive investment, etc.), the level of risk with the DST seems most linked to the deadly sins. Before proceeding, make sure to understand the offering and sponsor fully.

Photo 10 Sponsor: DeSanto Realty Group. Northwoods, Harrisburg, PA

Chapter 10

The LLC Placement
Smaller Equity Amounts, Non-1031 Investing,
IRA Placement
Adding an Asset to Your Balance Sheet

The LLC investment might be for you if:

- You are not in a 1031 tax-deferred exchange and have a smaller amount of cash you wish to invest (perhaps $25,000 or $50,000)

- You want to place some IRA or retirement funds into a TIC (only for qualified property programs) to diversify your portfolio

- You do not want to personally leverage but want a cash flow from real estate

Several TIC property offerings have this LLC component. Essentially, an LLC is formed as one of the tenants-in-common. You personally will not be on the property deed. You will be a member of the LLC. This is an all-cash position. The minimum amount can be as low as $25,000. (Sometimes, this amount could be even lower.)

You will complete a subscription agreement certifying that you are an accredited investor. You will sign an LLC agreement, but you will not complete the myriad other documents that TIC investors must complete, such as credit authorization, vesting instructions, or lender paperwork, which often relate to the financing. Some sponsors, but not all, require the last two years of tax forms.

Cons

There will probably be a fee split between you and the LLC administrator when the property is eventually sold later. (Most, but not all, sponsors do this.) This is compensation after the fact for administering the LLC. There may also be a small administration fee. Please read the LLC document and PPM carefully. Make sure you or your registered representative get the details on the program you are considering.

Some TIC sponsors that allow IRA funds may require a specific escrow holder to administer those funds, and there may be some fees involved in setting up the account or an annual fee charged by the trust company. If the TIC sponsor does not require a specific escrow holder, you may find that your current IRA custodian does not allow use of IRA funds for TICs. In this case, you would need to transfer your funds to another trustee or escrow provider to complete the transaction. This sometimes takes longer than you would expect, and there will probably be fees involved. Note that there could be some UBIT risk as well.

For the non-IRA investors, know that you will not be able to do a 1031 when the property eventually sells. You are not in a deeded ownership position of like-kind property. Instead, you are a member of an LLC. Your portion of the LLC is nontransferable and not liquid. If you are investing funds, they will stay invested for the duration of the property hold. (Most TICs state a five-to seven-year hold, but it can vary.)

As with the TIC and DST properties, the contracts, terms, and structures are nonnegotiable. These are prepackaged investments. There are the usual and typical risks involved. If the market goes soft, you might not sell when you expected, or you might not get the proceeds at sale that you hoped.

Pros

The LLC investment could be ideal for holding retirement funds because you will receive a monthly distribution into your retirement fund and can watch it grow consistently. Many mutual fund and stock investors have been dismayed over the last three years with slow growth. With an LLC position in a TIC or one of the alternatives, such as a note program, you normally have a relatively steady income, with the typical risks involved, of course. Some of the Note Programs are currently paying 8.5 to 9.5 percent annual returns.

The LLC can be good for those with smaller equity amounts who want passive income or perhaps want to diversify their portfolio with another type of income. Some investors use a small position in an LLC to get their feet wet before proceeding with a larger investment into a TIC or before adding an asset to their balance sheet. Post-closings into the LLC are often possible. This means a great TIC offering came and went and is closed out with TIC investors and is operating. Nevertheless, there is still room in the LLC for some investors for a period of time.

Other private placements that are not deeded real estate are also available in the private placement arena, such as note programs or real estate funds, oil and gas programs, equipment leasing programs, and other private placements. Some of the TIC sponsors offer such programs. The minimums on these programs can be as low as $25,000 or even less, even though some offerings require $100,000 minimums. Because they are private placements, all of the same Reg D rules apply. Investors must be accredited. There can be no advertising. The offering must be made by a PPM. There must be full disclosure.

If interested, talk to your registered representative about the choices. The returns are higher than some other investments, but the risks may be higher in some of the offerings. Some programs, like oil and gas, could give you excellent tax deductions and the possibility of high returns.

The author is invested in several LLC placements in TIC properties as well as several oil and gas programs.

Photos 11. Sponsor: Covington Realty Partners, LLC. Monte Lago Apartments, Houston, Texas.

Chapter 11

What Could Go Wrong?

Several of the following risks could occur to anyone who invests in any real estate, not just a TIC. However, some risks are specifically related to TICs. Every single investment has risk, and you must think about this before placing any of your hard-earned funds into any offering.

It is a bit unnerving to look at a chapter like this. If we looked at every single thing that could go wrong with any type of venture or investment, it would throw us into a panic. (If we thought of all the bad things that could happen to us in a given day, some of us would never want to leave the house.) For investors who have experience with real estate, they know the risks, the cycles, the ups and downs. They have probably experienced some downside over their investment life. Investors who may have experienced the syndicated general or limited partnerships of the 1980s may have a bad taste in their mouths about a syndicated investment, even if TICs are not exactly the same as the partnerships of old.

If you don't have real estate experience, you should know that regardless of how good a property seems and regardless of how much due diligence you do, unforeseen events occur. Your cash flow could be reduced, or it could even stop for a short or long time. No sponsor, investor, representative, or lender ever wants this to happen. But it can. It can, it has, and it will.

If the TIC interest is sold as a security, risks will be specified in the PPM, which includes some language required by the SEC. General risks will be listed, but every PPM will also have a laundry list of specific risks. This will include information concerning the particular offering and its story.

Because specific risks will be related to a specific property and will be disclosed in the PPM, the following are some of the more general risks. When you read the PPM on potential investments, pay attention to the specific risks, ask for explanations, and weigh the issues. Many of the risks may have a very small percentage chance of happening, but they must be pointed out. Others might have a higher percentage chance.

Certainly, the risk that most investors ask about is losing the cash flow. Cash flow is dependent upon the tenants and, to some degree, the management and sponsor. There have been a handful of instances in which cash flow has been reduced on a TIC investment, including periods of no distributions and there are some TICs that are distributing cash flow from the reserves. Reduced cash flow could occur when a major tenant or tenants departs a property without notice. Or a tenant could leave after the expiration of the lease, but it takes longer than expected to get a new tenant.

Make sure to review the cash flow proforma and see what occupancy/vacancy rates have been accounted for, and make sure to discuss if the proforma is conservative or aggressive as regards the tenants and cash flow.

Closing Risk

A sponsor could have a delay in closing on the property. Worse, the sponsor could lose the property and be unable to close. This is by no means a common occurrence, but it could be a risk for a 1031 tax-deferred exchanger.

If the sponsor already owns the property, delays or loss would not occur, or it would be highly unlikely. However, many sponsors do a simultaneous close. That is, they put the property under contract, conduct all due diligence, arrange the loan, and put substantial nonrefundable monies down. Then they close/buy the property at the same time that all TICs close/buy into the offering. Most sponsors have enough experience to know at what stage it is safe to offer the property for sale. (After all, thorough due diligence has been done so there should be no surprises.) However, there could be sponsors who are rushing to do the transaction and jump the gun.

Alternatively, some unexpected circumstance could arise. To date, the author is aware of a few delayed TIC closings, closing three or four weeks later than expected, but they did not jeopardize the 180-day deadline. These were due to late dropouts of investors, very late return of investor paperwork (signed and notarized), or a property title problem that needed to be cured. Recently, with the capital market shakeup, there have been some lender delays—and there could be closing risk. Consider investing in deals which are already owned by the sponsor to reduce this risk. In fact, some sponsors will hold several closes on a property to minimize the risk. The author is not aware of any TIC property that was subscribed and ready to close but then not closing and placing anyone in peril. Nevertheless, the fact that this could happen should remind you to identify more than one property and have backup options for a 1031 tax-deferred exchange.

Subscription Risk

You could be confirmed into a property by a sponsor but then told a week or two later that you didn't make it in and are on a wait list, or are not in at all. If you are past your forty-five day identification period and have no other properties identified or available to you, this could be devastating. I am aware of this situation occurring, even though in those instances the investors were able to get into another identified property. It is not common, but it is a risk nevertheless. The situation would probably occur with less-experienced sponsors. Make sure to identify more than one property, and try to subscribe early enough so you are definitively confirmed before the forty-five day ID period is over.

In another situation, you could be confirmed into a subscription, but the lender could boot you out. I know of a few instances when this has occurred. If the net worth of an investor is just at $1 million, there is an imbalance between the investor's net worth and acquisition amount, or some bankruptcy or recent legal issue caused concern, the lender has the right to not accept you. Having had a bankruptcy in the past does not mean you will be rejected though. If asked, be prepared to explain it. Make sure that you have backup properties in your forty-five day period to identify in case something like this occurs.

Cash Flow Risk

This is the risk that the most investors ask about and was discussed earlier in the chapter. This risk is one of the reasons why only accredited investors are allowed to invest, and why registered representatives must understand your overall financial situation. If you wanted to live exclusively on the income from a TIC property, you can see the damage that could occur to your situation if that income was reduced or lost. That is why suitability is important and why you should never invest if this will be your only income.

The fact is, a property could underperform and hence the cash flow payments could be lowered from the expectations, or perhaps no payment would come for a period. We know that having good tenants, reserves, insurance, and the best managers in place will be essential. However, if the economy worsens in general, the market softens, or there are problems in the particular market where the property is located, this situation could become an issue no matter what.

In other cases, a tenant could unexpectedly break a lease or not renew. You may have difficulties getting a new tenant. Keep in mind that while your TIC property will have a non-recourse loan, which means you are not personally responsible for the entire loan and are only at risk for your portion, there is indeed risk in any income-producing property that tenant vacancy could reduce cash flow to the point where all rent would go to debt service.

Also, a property could have a call. This would be related to underperformance of the property, but it could also relate to a natural disaster or unforeseen circumstances. In this case, the tenants-in-common could be asked to add capital or equity to the property.

Management Risk

A property manager could do a horrible job. You, as a tenants-in-common, will have the right to vote out or change a manager. In general, property managers are of a high level. They see this work as serious business and invest their time and efforts accordingly. However, poor managers could exist. You should pay attention to the quarterly (or monthly) property reports and ask questions. The management company should have a proven track record of success and strong experience. It should know how to handle tenants and keep them happy while keeping the asset in top shape. It should know if a tenant is in trouble and is thinking of breaking a lease. It should know how to deal with tenants that leave early or do not renew a lease. It should also know how to attract strong new tenants and negotiate the best terms for you, the owners. Your cash flow depends on the tenants in place. Of course, one of the reasons you invest in a TIC is because you do not want to do the hard work of management. Remember, a good management company is a strong, positive factor in your decision to invest in a TIC. A poor company is a risk and negative factor.

Refinancing Problems

The loan has come due, but the real estate market is such that you have not been able to sell the property and, hence, need to refinance. Interest rates may be higher than when you purchased, hence perhaps cash flow could be affected. Maybe there are fewer tenants in the property, and the loan to value will not be as good, or the lender will require some hold-backs or more reserves.

Cross-collaterization, while positive on some levels, could be devastating if one of the properties within the cross-collaterization fails. The cross-collaterization could be in a portfolio offering, or it could be in an overall guarantee on the property, loan, or lease.

Resale

You could receive an offer to resell the property, but some of the tenants-in-common do not want to sell. There are usually ways to handle this, and a good sponsor or manager will lead an orderly process to show the investors why (or why not) a sale would be beneficial. Most investors go into the offering with the idea of collecting income for some time and then selling at a profit. One hopes that all investors are of like mind on this issue. However, there could be disagreement on a sale. The TIC Agreement will usually allow the assenting investors to buy out the dissenting investor(s), and the sponsor may have the right to buy some interests as well. However, this doesn't guarantee a solution, and there is some risk.

Market Risk

Keep in mind that if the economy or real estate market goes soft for the asset class or geographic location of your TIC, it is possible it would take some time to sell the building or, if exiting early, your share. You may have to sell at a discount. Perhaps you couldn't find a buyer and may decide to hold the property until the market recovers, which could be for some years. Interest rates in the market could also have an effect. This is the same for any type of real estate.

Other

A sponsor could go out of business or go bankrupt, and they may have been the recourse party to the loan or the master lessee.

The SEC or IRS could update or change regulations.

Because TICs are relatively new and there is no developed secondary market, another challenge or risk could be valuation should you decide you want to exit the property early. Even though the appraisal of the whole property being sold to and by a TIC sponsor is straightforward, valuing an individual TIC interest several years later might not be so straightforward. Many believe an interest would most likely be sold at par (the amount you originally invested), even though it could be sold for more or even sold at a discount.

There will be other specific risks named in each PPM for each TIC property, as required for securities offerings. These will be as vague as "tax laws could change and adversely affect you" to "tenant rollover risk could leave the building 50 percent unoccupied in year 2008 if tenants do not renew."

Review the risk section of the PPM. Pick out any risks that seem excessive, and discuss them with the sponsor and your team. There may be reasonable explanations—or not. In any case, it is important to contemplate the risks and invest with your eyes wide open.

Photos 12. (Two views) Sponsor: CORE Realty Holdings, LLC. Westridge Executive Plaza, Valencia, California.

Chapter 12

Liquidity and Exit Strategy

TICs, like all real estate, are not liquid investments. Unlike stocks, CDs, bonds, and the like, you cannot decide today to cash out and have the funds tomorrow. Real estate takes longer to sell, even if there is a willing buyer and seller.

Investors should never place funds into a TIC that they wish to be liquid. All TIC investors should think of the investment as long-term, whether that means a three-year hold, a ten-year hold, or even longer. The investor should intend to hold his or her investment in the TIC property until the property sells in order to benefit from his or her pro rata share of the proceeds at sale. It seems that TIC investors understand this issue—to date, it has not been a deterrent, or vast amounts of equity would not have been invested.

There is not yet a developed secondary market for sales. However, an interesting statistic emerged at the 2005 TICA fall conference during the liquidity and exit strategy committee meeting. Among securitized TIC deals and more than 4,800 investors from 2001 to 2004, only ten investors in TIC properties exited early since 2002. That is from among the thousands of investors and millions of dollars of equity placed.[3] By the way, none of these exits were due to death. While most in the industry believe a secondary market may eventually develop, there hasn't been a great need or desire so far, especially because these are seen as long-term, private placement investments and are sold as such.

---

3. *Source: Manny Nogales, Omni Brokerage; sourced by an unscientific poll by contacting all securities sponsors. TICA Liquidity and Exit Strategy Committee. Fall 2005.*

In fact, if the securities-registered representatives, their Broker/Dealers, and the sponsors are doing their jobs, the fact that these investments are illiquid is made abundantly clear. Theoretically, the investors who do participate are well informed. Many of the investors are used to real estate investments, which are often long-term and always illiquid.

Most sponsors articulate a proposed exit strategy with the TIC property, which is most often five to seven years. Sometimes, they will clearly state a ten-year hold. Sometimes, they will say the market conditions may be such that they believe a shorter time frame (two years, for instance) is anticipated. This may be related to how the property was purchased, the loan terms, the tenant's leasing length or strategy, or the location.

What if an investor needs to liquidate due to divorce, financial situation, heir liquidation, or some other circumstance? Can you, an investor, sell your percentage interest? Yes, you can. This is real estate, and it can be sold. You, as a tenants-in-common, would first offer your share to your fellow tenants-in-common in the property. In fact, with a described procedure, the TIC Agreement usually stipulates that an investor must do this.

If none of your fellow investors wishes to buy your share, you could then talk to the sponsor and your registered representative. 1031 investors are always looking for replacement property. Quite possibly, a match could be found. Because this is your real estate, you can offer the property yourself, like placing a "For Sale" sign in front of your house. However, in any case, the new buyer must be an accredited investor and must also be approved by the lender, like you were approved at the time of your acquisition. The new investor may have to be approved by the tenants-in-common if the agreement stipulates this. Rev Proc 2002-22 guidelines regarding financing state that "restrictions on the right to transfer, partition, or encumber interests in the property that are required by a lender and that are consistent with customary commercial lending practices are not prohibited." Hence, lenders can include limitations designed to protect the investment. These can include:

- Prior approval before an investor transfers a TIC interest and before a new buyer can be accepted
- A specific holding period for larger investors
- A vote of other TIC investors agreeing to a sale

There will be a period when the new buyer's LLC will need to be formed and title work will need to be done for the sale. All of the documents you signed for closing will need to be handled for the new buyer. You will need to supply updated information on the asset to the buyer since a new PPM would not be published. Amendments to original documents would be required. For instance, the TIC Agreement includes a list of all investors, which would be amended.

The lender or sponsor may have a limited number of future transfers per deal stipulated. Very few understand what the associated costs of such a transfer may be until it happens, which would include loan assumption fee as well as costs for legal, closing, and title. In fact, the biggest questions about a developed secondary market right now seem to be costs, legal issues, assumption of the loan or right to transfer and the valuation issues.

There has been discussion on the sales price of the percentage interest and valuation. Many think a seller would probably sell at par, that is, the same equity amount they purchased. However, there may be a discounted price, or there could be negotiations for a higher price. The seller has to realize there will be closing costs and fees involved as well. If an interest is sold at par, the final proceeds will be less than par. It could be said that, while sponsors care about their investors, transfers are relatively difficult. (Most sponsors or representatives do not have the experience in this area.) A TIC transfer would be complex, time-consuming, and costly. It will involve dealing with the lender, Title Company, attorneys and others. It also includes updating legal documents or handling amendments to existing documents. This does not generate any profit, but it does involve costs. No commissions are built in for resales by the sponsor, so the buyer and/or seller may have to pay a broker or registered representative out of their pocket or build the fee into the sales price. Further, we already touched on the issues of valuation, which may be difficult. The original appraisal may be less valid if the resale occurs several years later.

Still, many do think a secondary market will eventually be in demand. Because the industry is still relatively new and the real estate has been strong, the need may not happen for some time. The demand for existing TIC interests could increase when new TIC offerings slow down because of soft markets and/or lower yields. Perhaps seasoned properties with a track record and high returns would be desirable and in demand, especially if the real estate yields continue to drop or do not move much.

For the moment, resales of TICs are uncharted territory, but there may be specific procedures and sources that develop.

As far as resales of the TIC property, several sponsors have now gone full circle with their properties. The average returns to date seem to fall in the 10% to 15% or even 20% return range. A few have been lower, and a few have been higher.

Photo 13. Sponsor: Triple Net Properties, LLC. One Nashville Place, Nashville, Tennessee.

Chapter 13

Recap: The Main Points
Pros and Cons
How Do I Prepare to Invest?

Let's review the basics on TIC properties. We have learned that the TIC business is a complex intermeshing of commercial real estate, securities laws and regulations, tax rulings, investments and finance.

Pros

- TICs have made the 1031 tax-deferred exchange easier, as the time and process to acquire them is streamlined and faster than most other real estate acquisitions.

- You will own deeded real estate with all of its tax benefits, but you will not have to manage it. You receive a monthly cash flow, and freedom of time.

- In most cases, you will "buy up" to a better asset class, an institutional-grade property.

- You can replace the debt for your 1031, and you will be leveraging your equity with non-recourse financing.

- If buying a securitized TIC, you will be provided with full due diligence information and full disclosure.

- If you have enough minimum equity, you can diversify your acquisitions.

- You can diversify your overall wealth portfolio. Real estate is a good diversification to your portfolio of mutual funds, stock, bonds, private placements, and business investments.
- You will receive effortless cash flow.

Cons

- The investment will not be liquid.
- There could be future market risks, or there could be a reduction or loss of your cash flow.
- There could be a capital call, or there could be future re-financing risks.
- You will be invested into a property with a group of people who are unknown to you and who may have different opinions about resale or management.
- You cannot refinance your own portion of the property.
- You will not be in management control of the property.
- You could lose your entire equity investment, in the worst case scenario.

Preparing to Invest

After all of your research and contemplation of the pros and cons, if you feel you might want to invest in a TIC, the following are some preparation tips:

1. If you are going to sell investment property, review the potential sale with your accountant, attorney, real estate agent, and/or financial planner. Calculate your potential capital gains. Consider if it makes sense to conduct a 1031 tax-deferred exchange. If so, determine your goals for the replacement property. If you want passive income and are considering a TIC, outline the most important goals for you—the type of asset you want, your minimum requirements on cash flow, the importance of capital preservation, diversity, the types of tenants you prefer, and other things of that nature.

2. Interview and find your QI, if you will be doing a 1031. Ideally, do this before you go into contract on your relinquished property. Make sure to time the sale and trade well. Don't have your forty-five day identification period fall at the same time as a three-week cruise.

3. Interview, talk with, and discuss your upcoming trade with several registered representatives to see with whom you have a fit. (If you choose someone who is also a real estate-licensed broker, he or she may have access to properly structured real estate offerings as well.)

Determine his or her level of experience and knowledge of TICs. Determine if he or she is a member of TICA, and review his or her commercial real estate knowledge. (Having several representatives stumbling over each other only creates confusion with sponsors and each other, and it could even involve a dispute.) Choose your representative and then focus on the task with him or her. Most of the representatives who specialize in TICs have the same offerings available, and they are working without compensation for you. They are only paid if and when you close on a property.

4. Prepare your personal paperwork. To do so, you should:

- Update your Personal Financial Statement (PFS), which the registered representative will need to show that you are an accredited investor. It also will be required by the lender and sponsor when you subscribe for the same reason. The PFS will also give a snapshot into the suitability requirement. The industry players must follow the Reg D rules to be sure that all investors are qualified and suitable. Many good registered representatives can help you with your PFS if you or your accountant do not have one.

- Make a copy of your last two years of tax returns. This is the lender requirement. You will be asked for this at time of subscription or shortly thereafter. Most Broker/Dealers are required to have this information on file as well as with the registered representatives. (Recently a few lenders have asked for three years of tax returns.)

- If you are buying your TIC in an entity, make a copy of your trust, LLC, or corporation papers. (You will acquire title in the same entity as for that you sold in a 1031 tax-deferred exchange.) The sponsor, registered representative, and lender will need to review it. One copy can usually be supplied to your registered representative. He or she will make copies for the other parties who require it.

- Make a copy of your driver's license. This is a Patriot Act requirement for identification verification.

- Keep a copy of your QI statement and all QI contact information. At subscription, you will be supplying the contact information of your QI, but some sponsors also ask for proof of the closing and amount of funds available. You will be in close contact with your QI during the trade.

5. Plan your timing. You need time to focus and study your replacement options. You also need to receive and read the hefty PPMs, complete subscription documents, and so forth. You need to be available for receipt of the closing documents, that is, to review, sign, and notarize before returning them in a very timely fashion. If you will be leaving the country during this period or are going on a cruise or business trip during the time you will be receiving the closing documents, try to rearrange the sale of your relinquished property so the timing works, or make alternate arrangements. TIC closing paperwork can be delivered to an alternate location, but this requires coordination. If you are leaving the country, consider a power of attorney. Realize that the 1031 time frames are short and you will be making important decisions for property that you will hold for some time. Make time for the process and be ready. It always takes longer than you think it will.

6. If you are not online and using e-mail and the Internet, arrange this now. It is almost impossible to conduct 1031 business and transmit important TIC information in a very timely fashion without online access. In the TIC industry and 1031 business, you and the sellers need information in a timely fashion. Basic information on currently available TICs could be outdated by the time you receive the information by regular mail, for instance. Many forms are transmitted via e-mail. Not only that, most TIC sponsors stay in touch with investors via e-mail updates. Many will offer access to information on your new asset through a Web site with a password.

Photos 14. (Two views) Sponsor: Passco Real Estate Enterprises, Inc. Alanza Place, Phoenix, Arizona.

Glossary of Terms

1031: the Internal Revenue Code (IRC) section 1031 addresses the tax-deferred exchange of like-kind property. A 1031 or 1031 tax-deferred exchange is the act of selling an investment property and placing the proceeds into another investment property through a qualified intermediary in order to defer capital gains tax.

accommodator: the qualified intermediary or accommodator. The party who handles the 1031 tax-deferred exchange funds, following rules set by the Treasury Department. See qualified intermediary.

accredited investor: as defined in Regulation D, individuals are defined as sophisticated investors if they have a minimum of $1 million net worth or salary of $200,000 in the last two years ($300,000 if married). Accreditation is necessary for investment into private placements or TICs.

appreciation: an increase in an asset's value.

boot: in a 1031 tax-deferred exchange, boot is anything of value exchanged that is not like-kind to the relinquished property. This is usually cash or mortgage debt used to equalize the transaction.

broker/dealer: any individual or firm in the business of buying and selling securities for itself and others. Broker/Dealers must register with the SEC, and they are members of the Financial Industry Regulatory Authority (FINRA). When acting as a broker, the Broker/Dealer executes orders on behalf of his or her client. When acting as a dealer, a Broker/Dealer executes trades or investments for his or her firm's own account.

capital call: whereby it could be required that each co-owner adds capital to the property.

cash flow, cash-on-cash return, yield: when you invest in an income-producing property, your cash flow is the income paid to you after expenses. Cash flow will be quoted as an annual percentage, such as a seven percent return on your equity (paid monthly). If you invested $500,000 into a TIC that starts with a seven percent annual cash flow return, you would receive $35,000 annually or $2,916.66 monthly.

capital gain: difference between the sales price of the relinquished property less the selling expenses and the adjusted basis of the property.

capitalization (cap) rate: one of the ways in which income-producing investment properties are compared. A capitalization (cap) rate is the annual net income divided by the sales price. Cap rates may be noted when discussing the acquisition price of an income and/or a NNN property.

Delaware Statutory Trust (DST): an unincorporated association created by a trust instrument for which property is deposited, managed, administered, and operated. A trustee administers the trust for the members or beneficiaries. DSTs are not TICs, but they are very similar.

due diligence: the diligence or studies that are conducted before deciding to purchase or acquire a property.

equity and debt, minimum equity required: equity is cash, or the cash portion of an acquisition. A certain amount of equity will be raised to close on a TIC, and the minimum equity required to invest by each investor will always be stated. The sales price or acquisition price is usually defined by both the debt and equity amounts.

exchange accommodator: the qualified intermediary, QI, or facilitator.

FEA: Federation of Exchange Accommodators. www.1031.org

Form 8824 for Like-Kind Exchanges: the IRS form you will file at tax time regarding the 1031 tax-deferred exchange.

fractional interests: the percentage interest held by each co-owner in a TIC property.

Howey decision: a Supreme Court decision in which it was determined that an investment contract is included in the definition of a security. An investment contract is defined as an investment of money into a common enterprise with the expectation of profits derived primarily from the effort of others. Because of this (and other rulings), many believe TICs are securities and should be sold as such.

ID period: one of the 1031 tax-deferred exchange rules. From the day you sell the relinquished property, you have forty-five days to identify the property or properties you wish to acquire in the tax-deferred exchange. The QI works with you on the ID procedures and deadlines.

institutional-grade: trophy properties of high standard, good design, and construction that are class A and large enough to merit the attention of institutional investors, such as pension funds, life insurance companies, foundations, endowments, foreign governments, and so forth. They are usually located in primary (or perhaps secondary) markets and a prime demographic location. They may have a name anchor tenant or tenants. They are considered to be less risky than other real estate due to the strength of the tenants, the construction, the location, and the street appeal.

institutional investors: the large money investors such as pension funds, life insurance companies, foundations, endowments, and foreign governments.

leverage: financing; one leverages his or her cash to buy a larger property than with cash only.

like-kind property: any valid investment property held for productive use in trade, business, or investment purposes that can be exchanged in a 1031 tax-deferred exchange for valid investment property.

liquidity: the ability of an asset to be converted into cash quickly.

LLC placement: a placement of funds into an LLC structure of an income-producing property or investment that is usually a private placement security. Some TIC properties have an LLC placement component whereby an investor can place funds with a much lower minimum (perhaps $25,000). He or she would be a member of the LLC, not a deeded owner of the property. He or she would not take on debt for the TIC property. It can work for some IRA and retirement fund placements. It usually produces monthly cash flow.

load: the front-end fees. Load is the markup paid at the outset of a private placement that does not contribute materially to the actual investment. Certain fees must be taken up front by regulation, not at the back-end or during the investment. These fees will be fully disclosed in the PPM.

NASD: National Association of Securities Dealers, now called FINRA (Financial Industry Regulatory Authority).

NNN: triple-net, refers to the lease of a tenant. In a NNN lease, the tenants pay for everything regarding the property including rent, taxes, insurance, maintenance, utilities, and so forth. The only landlord charge would be debt service, if there is a loan. NNN leases are common with single-tenant retail properties such as Applebee's, Burger King, Advance Auto, 7-Eleven, Walgreen's, and so forth. NNN or double net means the landlord would be responsible for the roof and structure (plus any other items mentioned in the lease) while the tenant is responsible for everything else except debt service. Some TIC tenants have NNN leases.

non-recourse loan: a loan whose terms include the lender agreeing that its sole remedy in the event of failure to repay will be to foreclose against the property securing the loan. TIC properties usually have non-recourse loans, meaning each investor is not responsible for the large overriding loan. They are only at risk for his or her portion. A recourse loan would be one whereby the person who borrowed money would be responsible for that loan and its payments, whether or not the tenant is in place and paying its rent.

non-recourse carve-outs: also known as the bad-boy carve-outs. The carve-outs are the bad acts that, if committed by an investor, cause him or her to lose his or her non-recourse status. The loan would become recourse to the investor committing the act. Bad-boy acts include physically hurting or destroying the property or committing fraud or intentional misrepresentation.

passive income: Income derived from business or real estate investments in which the individual is not actively involved. Income-producing real estate is a prime example of a passive income vehicle. The three types of income are earned income (salary), portfolio income (stocks and bonds), and passive income (real estate, LLCs, or limited partnerships).

percentage interest: in a TIC property, the investors will hold a percentage interest of the property, or fractional interest.

PPM: private placement memorandum, or offering memorandum. This is the book of disclosure regarding the TIC or DST offering. Private placements in securities, such as TICs, must disclose all information and may be offered for sale through the PPM only.

private placement: a direct offering of a security or securities to a limited number of sophisticated institutional investors or accredited investors, as defined in the SEC requirements for a Reg D offering.

qualified intermediary (QI): qualified intermediary. Also known as an exchange accommodator or facilitator. This is the professional provider of the required mechanics for a 1031 tax-deferred exchange. The use of a QI as an independent party to facilitate the exchange was established by Treasury regulations as a safe harbor. The QI cannot be a related party to the exchanger, must receive a fee, holds the funds in trust, and acquires the relinquished property while acquiring the replacement property and transfers it to the exchanger.

registered representative: the securities-licensed individual who will assist you in the acquisition of the TIC property or other securities or private placements. A registered representative is affiliated with a Broker/Dealer, which is, in turn, licensed by the SEC and NASD. The representative is subject to securities compliance, rules, and regulations. He or she is much like a buyer's broker in the real estate world.

Regulation D (Reg D): the SEC adopted Regulation D (Reg D) in April 1982, which set forth objectives and clearly stated rules for private placement exemptions. Under the Securities Act of 1933, any offer to sell securities must either be registered with the SEC or meet an exemption. Reg D lays out the basic rules for exemption (Rules 501 to 506).

relinquished property: property that is being sold by the exchanger in a 1031 tax-deferred exchange. (Formally called the down-leg property or may be called a Phase I property.)

replacement property: new property being acquired or the target property being bought by or identified to be purchased by the exchanger. (Formally called the upleg property or may be called a Phase II property.)

Rev Proc 2002-22: the IRS Revenue Procedure ruling that set forth the guidelines whereby a TIC would be recognized as real estate, not as a partnership. Hence, it could be used in a 1031 tax-deferred exchange.

SEC: the Securities and Exchange Commission. Because most TICs are sold as securities, regulation and compliance comes under SEC rules as well as NASD rules. The SEC is the primary federal agency for the securities industry.

Securities and Exchange Commission (SEC): the primary federal regulatory agency for the securities industry whose responsibility is to promote full disclosure and protect investors against fraudulent and manipulative practices in the securities markets.

Securities Investor Protection Corporation (SIPC): a nonprofit membership corporation established by Congress that insures securities and cash in customer accounts up to $500,000 (up to $100,000 in cash) in the event of brokerage bankruptcy.

shadow-anchored: a retail property next to a major retailer, such as Wal-Mart or a grocery store, which is not part of the property nor owned by the same party.

single-member entity LLC: a disregarded entity (flow-through or invisible for tax purposes) that isolates the asset and makes it bankruptcy-remote and adds liability protection. Many lenders use this entity for each investor into a TIC.

SPE LLC: single-purpose or special-purchase entity LLC. It is the same as the single-member entity LLC.

sponsor: the company that buys or ties up and prepares a property for sale as a TIC. The sponsor conducts the due diligence, negotiates the loan, has all legal documents prepared, etc. for the TIC acquisition sale. The sponsor may be a real estate company or an entrepreneurial company.

subscription: one subscribes to a TIC investment. The subscription process includes completing a subscription questionnaire, completing credit authorization materials, supplying tax returns and net worth statements, and supplying information on the 1031 tax-deferred exchange

syndicate, syndication: a group of individuals or companies together undertaking a project that would not be feasible to pursue alone. It usually refers to underwriting or a private placement. This group of individuals or companies joins for a limited investment purpose. Real estate syndicates create, buy, sell, and operate real estate investments.

Tenant in Common (TIC) property: a property in which two or more individuals hold undivided percentage ownership. While a TIC property could theoretically refer to any property held by tenants-in-common, a TIC property has evolved into being defined as an institutional-grade property offered by a sponsor to investors as a legally-prepared property structured to comply with the IRS Rev Proc 2002-22 for a 1031. Most TICs are offered as private placements in securities though a few are offered strictly as real estate-based.

tenants-in-common: the investors who hold co-ownership in a TIC property. A legal arrangement whereby two individuals or more can share undivided ownership of a property. Unlike joint tenancy, tenancy-in-common allows a deceased person's property or property share to be passed to his or her beneficiaries instead of to the other owner(s).

Tenant in Common Association (TICA): the active professional association comprised of securities broker/dealers, registered representatives, sponsors, attorneys, lenders, real estate professionals, title companies, and others who deal in the TIC industry (www.ticassoc.org).

TIC Agreement: the operating agreement that sets the rules and guidelines for the rights of ownership in each TIC property. The agreement explains which decisions must be unanimous in vote, how to handle the manager and management agreement on the property, inspection of books and records, right of first refusal, and other important issues.

TIC best practices memo: established players in the TIC industry wish to standardize practices among all players for ethical and fair dealing and to ensure the industry is not tarnished by new players or experienced players not following the rules. This is not a static document and is a work in progress.

Photo 15. LLC. Mapleridge Shopping Center, Mapleridge (St. Paul) MN.